LifeLight

"In Him was life, and the life was the light of men." John 1:4

Life of David

LEADERS GUIDE

CONCORDIA PUBLISHING HOUSE • SAINT LOUIS

From the study:

Many people remember David as the Israelite who killed Goliath the giant. Or as the good friend of Jonathan. Or as the king who committed adultery with Bathsheba. If these things are all we remember, David's life gets distorted. This LifeLight Bible study is concerned with rendering an accurate portrayal of David. But even more important, we will study the events of David's life that the Lord God had recorded for us so that *our* lives will not be judged, so we can instead delight in the mercy that God now shows us in the Son of David, Jesus Christ.

Dutch painter Jan Victors (1619-1676) frequently painted Bible scenes. Here, "Samuel Anointing David" shows participants wearing clothing of the artist's era. Thanks be to God that Christ, our Spirit-anointed Savior, took our sins to the cross and, in Baptism, clothed us with His perfect righteousness.

Copyright © 1998, 2010 Concordia Publishing House
3558 S. Jefferson Ave., St. Louis, MO 63118-3968
1-800-325-3040 • www.cph.org

All rights reserved. No part of this publication may be reproduced, stored in a retrieval system, or transmitted, in any form or by any means, electronic, mechanical, photocopying, recording, or otherwise, without the prior written permission of Concordia Publishing House.

Written by Joel A. Brondos and Donna Streufert

Edited by Ken Schurb

Field testing coordinated by Rev. Eric Van Scyoc, St. Thomas Lutheran Church, Rocky River, OH

Cover illustration: *Samuel Anointing David*, Staatliche Kunstsammlung Kassel, Germany/SuperStock

Scripture quotations are from the ESV Bible® (The Holy Bible, English Standard Version®), copyright © 2001 by Crossway Bibles, a publishing ministry of Good News Publishers. Used by permission. All rights reserved.

Quotations marked *LSB* are from *Lutheran Service Book*, copyright © 2006 Concordia Publishing House. All rights reserved.

Quotations from Luther's Small Catechism are copyright © 1986 Concordia Publishing House. All rights reserved.

The quotation from Luther's Works is from the American Edition: vol. 15, © 1972 by Concordia Publishing House. All rights reserved.

This publication may be available in braille, in large print, or on cassette tape for the visually impaired. Please allow 8 to 12 weeks for delivery. Write to Lutheran Blind Mission, 7550 Watson Rd., St. Louis, MO 63119-4409; call toll-free 1-888-215-2455; or visit the Web site: www.blindmission.org.

Manufactured in the United States of America

1 2 3 4 5 6 7 8 9 10   19 18 17 16 15 14 13 12 11 10

Contents

Introducing the LifeLight Program		5
Session 1—Lecture Leader	A Messianic Mountaintop 1 Samuel 16:1–13; Psalm 23; Psalm 110	8
Session 2—Lecture Leader	David on the Field 1 Samuel 16–18	12
Session 3—Lecture Leader	David on the Run 1 Samuel 19–31	16
Session 4—Lecture Leader	David on the Rise 2 Samuel 1:1–5:5	21
Session 5—Lecture Leader	David on the Throne 2 Samuel 5:6–10:19	25
Session 6—Lecture Leader	David on the Edge 2 Samuel 11:1–12:31	30
Session 7—Lecture Leader	David under the Sword 2 Samuel 13:1–22:51	34
Session 8—Lecture Leader	David at the Last 2 Samuel 23:1–1 Kings 2:46	38
Session 9—Lecture Leader	David's Son, David's Lord Selected Passages	42
Session 1—Small-group Leader	A Messianic Mountaintop 1 Samuel 16:1–13; Psalm 23; Psalm 110	49
Session 2—Small-group Leader	David on the Field 1 Samuel 16–18	52
Session 3—Small-group Leader	David on the Run 1 Samuel 19–31	56
Session 4—Small-group Leader	David on the Rise 2 Samuel 1:1–5:5	60
Session 5—Small-group Leader	David on the Throne 2 Samuel 5:6–10:19	63
Session 6—Small-group Leader	David on the Edge 2 Samuel 11:1–12:31	66
Session 7—Small-group Leader	David under the Sword 2 Samuel 13:1–22:51	69
Session 8—Small-group Leader	David at the Last 2 Samuel 23:1–1 Kings 2:46	73
Session 9—Small-group Leader	David's Son, David's Lord Selected Passages	76

Introduction

Welcome to LifeLight

A special pleasure is in store for you. You will be instrumental in leading your brothers and sisters in Christ closer to Him who is our life and light (John 1:4). You will have the pleasure of seeing fellow Christians discover new insights and rediscover old ones as they open the Scriptures and dig deep into them, perhaps deeper than they have ever dug before. More than that, you will have the pleasure of sharing in this wonderful study.

LifeLight—An In-depth Study

LifeLight is a series of in-depth Bible studies. The goal of LifeLight is that through a regular program of in-depth personal and group study of Scripture, more and more Christian adults may grow in their personal faith in Jesus Christ, enjoy fellowship with the members of His body, and reach out in love to others in witness and service.

In-depth means that this Bible study includes the following four components: individual daily home study; discussion in a small group; a lecture presentation on the Scripture portion under study; and an enhancement of the week's material (through reading the enrichment magazine).

LifeLight Participants

LifeLight participants are adults who desire a deeper study of the Scriptures than is available in the typical Sunday morning adult Bible class. (Mid-to-older teens might also be LifeLight participants.) While LifeLight does not assume an existing knowledge of the Bible or special experience or skills in Bible study, it does assume a level of commitment that will bring participants to each of the nine weekly assemblies having read the assigned readings and attempted to answer the study questions. Daily reading and study will require from 15 to 30 minutes for the five days preceding the LifeLight assembly. The day following the assembly will be spent reviewing the previous week's study by going over the completed study leaflet and the enrichment magazine.

LifeLight Leadership

While the in-depth process used by LifeLight begins with individual study and cannot achieve its aims without this individual effort, it cannot be completed by individual study alone. Therefore, trained leaders are necessary. You fill one or perhaps more of the important roles described below.

The Director

This person oversees the LifeLight program in a local center (which may be a congregation or a center operated by several neighboring congregations). The director

- serves as the parish LifeLight overall coordinator and leader;
- coordinates the scheduling of the LifeLight program;
- orders materials;
- convenes LifeLight leadership-team meetings;
- develops publicity materials;
- recruits participants;
- maintains records and budgeting;
- assigns, with the leadership team, participants to small discussion groups;
- makes arrangements for facilities;
- communicates outreach opportunities to small-group leaders and to congregational boards;
- follows up on participants who leave the program.

The Assistant Director *(optional)*

This person may assist the director. Duties listed for the director may be assigned to the assistant director as mutually agreeable.

The Lecture Leader

This person prepares and delivers the lecture at the weekly assembly. **(Lesson material for the lecture leader begins on p. 9.)** The lecture leader

- prepares and presents the Bible study lecture to the large group;

- prepares worship activities (devotional thought, hymn, prayer), using resources in the study leaflet and leaders guide and possibly other, outside sources;
- helps the small-group discussion leaders to grow in understanding the content of the lessons;
- encourages prayer at weekly leadership-team and discussion leaders meetings.

The Small-Group Coordinator *(optional; the director may fill this role)*

This person supervises and coordinates the work of the small-group discussion leaders. The small-group coordinator

- recruits with the leadership-team the small-group discussion leaders;
- trains or arranges for training of the discussion leaders;
- assists the director and discussion leaders in follow-up and outreach;
- encourages the discussion leaders to contact absent group members;
- participates in the weekly leadership-team and discussion-leaders equipping meetings;
- provides ongoing training and support as needed.

The Small-Group Discussion Leaders

These people guide and facilitate discussion of Life-Light participants in the small groups. **(Lesson material for the small-group leaders begins on p. 49.)** There should be one discussion leader for every group of no more than twelve participants. The small-group discussion leaders are, perhaps, those individuals who are most important to the success of the program. They should, therefore, be chosen with special care and be equipped with skills needed to guide discussion and to foster a caring fellowship within the group. These discussion leaders

- prepare each week for the small-group discussion by using the study leaflet and small-group leaders guide section for that session;
- read the enrichment magazine as a study supplement;
- guide and facilitate discussion in their small group;
- encourage and assist the discussion group in prayer;
- foster fellowship and mutual care within the discussion group;
- attend weekly discussion-leaders training meetings.

Leadership Training

LifeLight leaders will meet weekly to review the previous week's work and plan the coming week. At this session, leaders can address concerns and prepare for the coming session. LifeLight is a 1½-hour program with no possibility for it to be taught in the one hour typically available on Sunday mornings. Some congregations, however, may want to use the Sunday morning Bible study hour for LifeLight preparation and leadership training. In such a meeting, the lecture leader and/or small-group coordinator may lead the discussion leaders through the coming week's lesson, reserving five or ten minutes for problem solving or other group concerns.

While it requires intense effort, LifeLight has proven to bring great benefit to LifeLight participants. The effort put into this program, both by leaders and by participants, will be rewarding and profitable.

The LifeLight Weekly Schedule

Here is how LifeLight will work week by week:

1. Before session 1, each participant will receive the study leaflet for session 1 and the enrichment magazine for the course. The study leaflet contains worship resources (for use both in individual daily study and at the opening of the following week's assembly) and readings and study questions for five days. Challenge questions will lead those participants who have the time and desire a greater challenge into even deeper levels of study.

2. After the five days of individual study at home, participants will gather for a weekly assembly of all Life-Light participants. The assembly will begin with a brief period of worship (5 minutes). Participants will then join their assigned small discussion groups (of twelve or fewer, who will remain the same throughout the course), where they will go over the week's study questions together (55 minutes). Assembling together once again, participants will listen to a lecture presentation on the readings they have studied in the previous week and discussed in their small groups (20 minutes). After the lecture presentation, the director or another leader will distribute the study leaflet for the following week.

Closing announcements and other necessary business may take another five minutes before dismissal.

In some places, some small groups will not join the weekly assembly because of scheduling or other reasons. Such groups may meet at another time and place (perhaps in the home of one of the small group's members). Those congregations may record the lecture given by the lecture leader at the weekly assembly and duplicate it for use by other groups meeting later in the week.

3. On the day following the assembly, participants will review the preceding week's work by rereading the study leaflet they completed (and that they perhaps supplemented or corrected during the discussion in their small group) and by reading appropriate articles in the enrichment magazine.

Then the LifeLight weekly study process will begin all over again!

Recommended Study Resources and Worship

The Lutheran Study Bible, English Standard Version. St. Louis: Concordia Publishing House, 2009 (order 01-2030). The first English Bible to be developed with distinctively Lutheran study notes, this comprehensive, devotional edition includes application notes, cross-references, timelines, prayers, full-color maps, charts, diagrams, and over 220 articles and introductions to Bible books.

Concordia Self-Study Bible, New International Version. St. Louis: Concordia Publishing House, 1986. Interpretive notes on each page form a running commentary on the text. The book includes cross-references, a 35,000-word concordance, full-color maps, charts, and timelines.

Roehrs, Walter R., and Martin H. Franzmann. *Concordia Self-Study Commentary*. St. Louis: Concordia Publishing House, 1979. This one-volume commentary on the Bible contains 950 pages and is tailored for lay use.

Every Voice a Song Pipe Organ Accompaniment for 180 Hymns and Liturgy. St. Louis: Concordia Publishing House (order no. 99-1565). Use this music CD for worship hymn accompaniment.

Lecture Leaders Session 1 | Life of David

A Messianic Mountaintop

1 Samuel 16:1–13; Psalm 23; Psalm 110

Preparing for the Session

Central Focus

God's plan of salvation proceeded through many generations from Adam to Christ. The life of David serves as one of the messianic mountaintops from which the whole range of God's work in Christ can be seen.

Objectives

That participants, led by the Holy Spirit working through God's Word, will

1. acquire a general overview of what is to come before embarking on a more detailed study of David's life;

2. appreciate the extraordinary circumstances of David's life—as well as the extraordinary means by which God sustained and protected David; and

3. examine their own lives in order to prepare them for the message of Law and Gospel proclaimed through God's dealings with David.

Note for the small-group leaders: Lesson notes and other materials you will need begin on page 57.

For the Lecture Leader

You have a key role in this Bible study. Your weekly presentation will sum up the study that has gone on all week, by the participants both individually and also in their small-group discussions. Because your part is so important, plan to devote proper time and attention in preparing your presentation each week.

Luther taught that prayer, meditation, and struggle make a theologian. As a presenter, you will be serving as a theologian for your hearers, directing them into the Word of Christ. Begin with prayer. You might draw from some of the prayers found in the front of your hymnal. Find additional material for your prayers as you reflect on portions of Psalm 110.

Next, meditate. Don't merely rely on this Leaders Guide. Read and study God's Word yourself. There are two important reasons to do so:

First, God's Word is living and active, bestowing His Spirit of truth and life.

Second, God's words are better than your words. You are not asking your hearers to take you at your word, but to let God establish them firmly upon the witness of the prophets and apostles. Let the daily assignments and study questions lead you into that Word for your own meditation and as you prepare to lecture.

Finally, expect some "struggles" with the text and in your own life as you prepare each presentation. Anticipate what portions of the lesson may be difficult for those who will gather to hear and discuss it. Difficulties may range from the pronunciation of biblical names to just staying attentive after a long day in the battle all God's people wage against Satan, sin, and their own flesh.

If possible, present the material in your own words, using the printed lecture as a guide. Maintain eye contact with the class members. If you do read the printed lecture, practice several times so that you are thoroughly familiar with it. You need not stick to the printed text, word for word. Your own illustrations and applications may fit your situation or audience better than what appears here. Keep in mind, however, that a sharp focus on the main points of the printed lecture will best help the class members see the connections between the study leaflet they prepare before the class, your presentation, and the review material they study after class each week.

Session Plan

Worship

Begin the session with the hymn printed in the study leaflet. Accompaniments are available in denominational hymnals, such as *Lutheran Service Book* or *Lutheran Worship* (refer to hymnal index). (Note: Concordia Publishing House has available *Every Voice a Song*, a nine-CD set of organ accompaniments for 180 hymns and liturgy. All the initial worship hymns in the Life-Light courses are included in this resource. It's especially helpful for mission congregations and small parishes. See the list of study resources on p. 7.) Follow with this prayer:

Prayer

Lord God, as we begin this study of the life of Your servant David, cleanse our hearts and minds so that we might be receptive to Your Word. As we learn more about David, draw us closer to Your Son, Jesus Christ, David's son and David's Lord. We ask this in His name. Amen.

Lecture Presentation

Introduction

What events in your life do other people remember most? The winning basket you made in a playoff game? The time you won high honors? A mistake you made? Such occasions were significant events in your past, but they may not really give a proper perspective of your life as a whole. They can get blown out of proportion. They may be brought up again and again—to your embarrassment—by Uncle Fred or Aunt Ellen at your annual family gathering. At such times, you wish that people would just forget about such things and get to know you as you really are now.

Many people remember David as the Israelite who killed Goliath the giant. Or as the good friend of Jonathan. Or as the king who committed adultery with Bathsheba. If these things are all we remember, David's life gets distorted. This LifeLight Bible study is concerned with rendering an accurate portrayal of David. But even more important, we will study the events of David's life that the Lord God had recorded for us so that *our* lives will not be judged, so we can instead delight in the mercy that God now shows us in the Son of David, Jesus Christ.

1 Larger than Life

What happened in David's life began centuries before his birth. It would continue to unfold in the centuries after his death. The apostles Peter and Paul both noted David's significance. On the Day of Pentecost, Peter quoted from Psalm 16 and from Psalm 110—both written by David. These psalms played an essential part in Peter's defense of the Gospel and allowed him to conclude, (Acts 2:36) "Let all the house of Israel therefore know for certain that God has made Him both Lord and Christ, this Jesus whom you crucified."

Likewise, the church of Pisidian Antioch invited Paul to speak a message of encouragement for the people. In response, Paul laid out God's plan of salvation from the exodus to Christ. In a key portion of that message, he made reference to David: (Acts 13:23) "Of this man's [David's] offspring God has brought to Israel a Savior, Jesus, as He promised." And again: (Acts 13:36–37) "For David, after he had served the purpose of God in his own generation, fell asleep and was laid with his fathers and saw corruption, but He whom God raised up did not see corruption."

On one hand, the life of David was simply not big enough to stage the Lord's entire production of salvation in Jesus Christ. But on the other hand, no account of redemption would be complete without a full reference to David. As we delight in the Gospel, we long to hear the whole story of how the Lord accomplished so great a salvation for us. David's life forms an important part of that "whole story." How can we help but marvel at *all* the details and nuances of God's plan that ultimately came together in the crucifixion and resurrection of Jesus? Like the Jews in Acts 2:37 who were "cut to the heart," this full message leads us to daily repentance. It calls us to remember Holy Baptism, through which Christ's history has become our history. Like the Gentiles in Acts 13:48 who were glad to hear the Good News and who honored the Word of the Lord, we spread this same history through whole regions of our world too as God fills us with joy and the Holy Spirit.

2 A King Too Soon

The Lord God had always planned to establish a king for His people. Some three hundred years before the Israelites anointed their first king, the Lord God had spoken to Moses as the children of Israel wandered in the wilderness: "When you come to the land that the Lord your God is giving you, and you possess it and dwell in it and then say, 'I will set a king over me, like all the nations that are around me,' you may indeed set a king over you whom the Lord your God will choose. One from among your brothers you shall set as king over you" (Deuteronomy 17:14–15a).

The King of God's choosing, Jesus Christ, was not yet available when the Israelites asked Samuel to appoint a king (1 Samuel 8:4–9). The request did not synchronize with the timetable of God's gracious will. The world had not yet arrived to what Paul (Galatians 4:4) called "the fullness of time." The people had not sought the Lord's counsel in this matter. Instead, they imposed their own counsel on God's spokesman, the prophet Samuel, and thus upon the Lord Himself, by demanding a king. They wanted a king, and they wanted one now!

Who, then, could be hurriedly anointed into this position if the Lord's Anointed One, the Messiah, was not yet to be found upon the earth? Saul appeared a likely candidate. He was "a handsome young man. There was not a man among the people of Israel more handsome than he. From his shoulders upward he was taller than any of the people" (1 Samuel 9:2). He was the first king of Israel, anointed by Samuel and acclaimed by the people when he rescued the city of Jabesh Gilead. Saul, however, did not live up to the high hopes of the people. He proved himself to be much like the people he led—foolish, rash, and irreverent. Because of Saul's repeated disobedience and his hardness of heart, the Lord rejected Saul as king, even though, as we shall see, many in Israel remained loyal to Saul in the years that followed.

This slice of Israelite history illustrates the truth that impatience with other people may actually disguise our impatience with God. When the Israelites asked Samuel to anoint a king for them, they seemed to have good reasons. The sons of Samuel had grown as dishonest and wicked as the sons of the priest Eli had been in the years before Samuel's rise to leadership. Samuel had no apparent successors. Who would lead and judge the Israelites with wisdom and integrity? We can sympathize with the people's concern.

When things are not getting done as quickly or as well as we would like in our own lives or in our own congregation, don't we often tend to take matters into our own hands? At such times, we would do well to consider the means the Lord has ordained and established for accomplishing His work. If we insist on immediate solutions, we may be leaving ourselves open for the same kind of subsequent disappointment the Israelites experienced with Saul.

The period typified by the reign of Israel's earthly kings, from Saul to Zedekiah, lasted about five hundred years. It ended with Assyrian brutality and Babylonian captivity. The Lord God had warned His people that disobedience would result in dire consequences: (Deuteronomy 28:33–37) "A nation that you have not known shall eat up the fruit of your ground and of all your labors, and you shall be only oppressed and crushed continually, so that you are driven mad by the sights that your eyes see. The LORD will strike you on the knees and on the legs with grievous boils of which you cannot be healed, from the sole of your foot to the crown of your head. The LORD will bring you and your king whom you set over you to a nation that neither you nor your fathers have known. And there you shall serve other gods of wood and stone. And you shall become a horror, a proverb, and a byword among all the peoples where the LORD will lead you away."

During the many centuries before King Saul, the people of Israel had been governed and guided by patriarchs, judges, and prophets. The individuals who occupied these offices failed to stem the tide of sin. They failed to bring the nation to produce true righteousness and lasting faithfulness. Not a single one of them, nor the whole lot together, could stop Israel from accumulating a huge account with a cruel taskmaster. Sin, you see, pays its wages—death. The "wages" we had accumulated could be wiped out only by the Lord Himself on the day He would fulfill His Gospel promise to Adam, to Abraham, and to all His old covenant nation. That day drew nearer when Samuel anointed David to be Israel's second king, Saul's replacement.

3 From Pasture to Palace

What kind of man was David? You already may have an opinion. Was he a compulsive, passionate young man who had a hard time growing into maturity? Was he a wise, God-fearing hero? Was he simply a human being with ordinary faults who found himself caught up in the extraordinary events surrounding God's purposes in earth's history?

David did not volunteer for his position in divine history. His older brothers called him in from the pasture to meet someone named Samuel, who anointed him with oil in the presence of those brothers. This anointing, done in secret for fear of Saul, indicated God's choice of David as King Saul's successor. The events that followed this anointing propelled David onward. He gained fame by defeating Goliath. Admiration stirred in the hearts of the people because of that victory, while jealousy curdled the heart of Saul. When King Saul's jealousy gave birth to violence, David had to run for his life. As a refugee, he found that "desperate times call for desperate measures." Together with a band of followers that eventually numbered more than six hundred, David was compelled to take advantage of resources and strategies that people who are well-established in their homes and communities (like our own) never have to use. Saul kept trying to run David through with a spear. But that spear eventually pierced Saul's own heart as he fell on it, committing suicide on Mount Gilboa.

David did not immediately take the throne at Saul's death. Ishbosheth, a son of Saul, claimed the crown as Saul's rightful heir. (Jonathan, David's friend and Saul's firstborn, died in the same battle as King Saul.) The Promised Land was for a time divided temporarily—as it later would be permanently—into two rival peoples, Israel to the north and Judah to the south; Ishbosheth to the north and David to the south. Against David's wishes, his rivals in the north were eventually murdered. David nonetheless was able to unite the kingdom. He conquered the mountain fortress called Jerusalem, making this city home—both to his palace and to the ark of the covenant.

Living in a splendid palace himself, David thought the ark of the covenant should be housed in equal splendor. What pleased the Lord, however, was not that David build a magnificent temple, but that He Himself, the Lord, build an eternal throne for David, a dynasty. From this dynasty would come the ultimate King, King Jesus, the Messiah who would save His people from their sins.

What more could the Lord have done for David? And yet the sinful heart can deceive even someone like King David, even someone like you or like me. In selfishness, our hearts focus too often on satisfying our own desires, our lust for power, for position, for recognition. Or, in David's case, a lust for pleasure.

David's sexual lust led him into his darkest days. He became an adulterer and a murderer. The Lord forgave David. And yet the prophet Nathan, who pronounced God's absolution, also warned David that his sins would result in earthly consequences that could not be annulled. David's sins brought terrible strife and sorrow down upon his household. One of his sons raped one of his daughters. When David did nothing, another son—Absalom—took revenge for his sister's rape, killing the guilty brother and seizing his father's throne by guile and power. David survived this rebellion and regained his throne, only to have a bloody civil war break out once again. Yet another son—Adonijah—presumed to take the throne in place of his aging father, but through the intrigue of the prophet Nathan and David's wife Bathsheba, David overcame this challenge and established Solomon as his successor. Soon after, David died and was buried in Jerusalem.

Would you want to be like David? Perhaps the idea of living out the role of a heroic giant-killer or that of a glorious king appeals to you. But this was not the purpose for which the Lord God recorded David's life in the Holy Scriptures. We do a great disservice to the Lord when we call to mind only the short-lived high points of David's career. Similarly, we miss the point when we imagine our own time to be more civilized, more "Christian" than the days and kingdom of David. The inspired history recorded for us in the Holy Scriptures was not written so that we could take comfort in our own supposed virtue. No, it was recorded to reveal our God as the most gracious Lord. Yes, we want to be like David—not in terms of the lurid details of his life, but in terms of the grace and mercy promised to him through the One who would one day be established on David's throne forever: Jesus Christ, David's Son and David's Lord.

Conclusion

If you've ever followed a daytime soap opera or an ongoing evening drama on television, you know how complicated the plots can get. The life of David is every bit as dramatic and complex as any soap opera. The details of his life may seem difficult to follow at times, but don't get discouraged. Simply take note of how easily and thoroughly a life can become entangled in sin and engulfed in sin's consequences.

In the same way, this portion of salvation history will appear every bit as violent and vulgar as any R-rated movie or romance novel, but don't be disturbed. None of the atrocities committed by human beings kept the Lord from accomplishing His good and gracious purposes in Christ.

Keep in mind, too, that the very same Lord who brought David through *his* eventful life also knows how to rescue *you*, no matter how complex your life may become, no matter how guilty you are. The cross of Christ and the Savior who died there have removed your sin and mine. We can come to Him in repentance and faith, certain of His mercy. We can receive from Him the power to remove the sin that stains us and the chains of sin that enslave us.

Concluding Activities

Pray a prayer that flows from the words of Psalm 1:6, "For the Lord knows the way of the righteous, but the way of the wicked will perish."

Then distribute Study Leaflet 2. Make any necessary announcements before you dismiss the group.

Lecture Leaders Session 2 | Life of David

David on the Field

1 Samuel 16–18

Preparing for the Session

Central Focus

The Lord delivers His people in unusual and remarkable ways. In times past and still today, God chooses and uses unlikely people—sinners, all—to accomplish His purposes.

Objectives

That participants, led by the Holy Spirit working through God's Word, will

1. see that God works in surprising ways;

2. develop a stronger confidence in God when threatened;

3. do everything—in word and deed—in the name of the Lord; and

4. trust God's work on their behalf in Christ.

Note for the small-group leaders: Lesson notes and other materials you will need begin on page 60.

For the Lecture Leader

When attempting to relate any portion of history, it is sometimes difficult to know where to begin. A study on the life of David could well begin with 1 Samuel 1. Instead, we have chosen to arrive on the textual scene some 16 chapters into the account.

As you teach this lesson, keep in mind that the life of David begins well before the events recorded in 1 Samuel 16. But Scripture does not record his birth or childhood. That's because David's life is being told from the perspective of salvation history. In one sense, the life of David begins with the creation of human beings and the promise God made to Adam and Eve to send a Savior after the fall (Genesis 3:15). David follows in the line of all those in Israel whose lives point to the coming Christ.

As you prepare for this session, you might read the earlier chapters of 1 Samuel. In a quiet place, reflect on what the Lord, the God of Abraham, Isaac, and Jacob, has done thus far in the history of the children of Israel. You may want to use the summaries of all this recorded for us in Psalm 78 or Hebrews 11. Take this rich context with you into your study of David's life, and be on the lookout for themes of Law and Gospel, sin and grace, that recur throughout the Scriptures.

Session Plan

Worship

Begin the session with the hymn printed in the study leaflet. Accompaniments are available in denominational hymnals, such as *Lutheran Service Book* or *Lutheran Worship* (refer to hymnal index). (Note: Concordia Publishing House has available *Every Voice a Song*, a nine-CD set of organ accompaniments for 180 hymns and liturgy. All the initial worship hymns in the Life-Light courses are included in this resource. It's especially helpful for mission congregations and small parishes. See the list of study resources on p. 7.) Follow with this prayer:

Prayer

Heavenly Father, You selected David to be Your servant king over Your people, Israel. Help us to accept your call on our lives as we serve our neighbors in love and as we draw strength from our Suffering Servant, King Jesus. In His name we pray. Amen.

Lecture Presentation

Introduction

Deep, bitter feelings often develop when someone is rejected. The United States Postal Service and, unfortunately, other businesses as well, have learned by sad, violent experience that fired employees often harbor resentment, even if they deserved to be dismissed. We are about to see how David came to be king because Saul proved himself unworthy of that high position. Saul's bitterness and political maneuvering could not stop the Lord's determination to move forward His plan for the world's salvation in Christ.

Samuel had confronted Saul with his sins of disobedience, rebellion, and arrogance. Saul had not been faithful. Samuel told him, (1 Samuel 13:13-14) "You have done foolishly. You have not kept the command of the Lord your God, with which He commanded you. For then the Lord would have established your kingdom over Israel forever. But now your kingdom shall not continue. The Lord has sought out a man after His own heart, and the Lord has commanded him to be prince over His people, because you have not kept what the Lord commanded you."

A short time later, Samuel proclaimed the most bitter words Saul was ever to hear: "Because you have rejected the word of the Lord, He has also rejected you from being king" (1 Samuel 15:23b). This rejection took a heavy toll on Saul. Murderous rage soon filled his heart.

Saul's rejection led to David's election. David was the "man after [God's] own heart" about whom Samuel spoke. The Lord called David this *before* David had done any of the noble works recorded in the Scriptures. It's important that we note this. David was a "man after [God's] heart" because of the Lord's gracious favor and not because of David's deeds. David didn't merit the Lord's favor by displaying heroic character time after time. Rather, the Lord strengthened David's heart, enabling him to accomplish wonderful things even in the presence of fearsome enemies.

1 From Rejection to Election (16:1-13)

The prophet Samuel had anointed Saul to be king, but Saul turned out to be a terrible disappointment despite Samuel's prayers and admonitions. The Lord finally abandoned Saul; He withdrew His Spirit from Saul in a last-ditch effort to awaken him to the grave, the mortal danger his sin posed. But Saul plunged headlong into further disobedience and rebellion. Samuel mourned for him.

When the Lord told Samuel to anoint a new candidate for the throne, Samuel's grief gave way to fear. Samuel knew that Saul well might strike out in anger and frustration. And Samuel said, (v. 2) "How can I go? If Saul hears it, he will kill me."

The Lord dealt with Samuel's fear by giving him a secondary task that seemed less daunting: take a heifer to Bethlehem for sacrifice. Some treat this command as though God were giving Samuel a little white lie to hide behind, a bit of subterfuge so Samuel could sneak under Saul's nose without arousing his ire. Such an idea runs contrary to the dignity of our Lord. More likely, the Lord gave Samuel a small task with which he could begin. It's often easier to start an unpleasant task by doing the least difficult part. This sacrifice was not superfluous. It served both to lessen Samuel's fear and to calm those he was about to visit.

Verses 4-5—The fearful prophet traveled to Bethlehem and met fearful inhabitants. The elders of the town trembled when they met him. "Do you come peaceably?" they asked him. People may experience a similar kind of fear when they see the flashing lights of a police car behind them. Does the officer come to protect or to punish—to warn that the right rear wheel is about to fall off or to give a ticket for speeding? Church members have sometimes felt a similar kind of reticence when the pastor or an elder visits their home unexpectedly. As they answer the door with pounding hearts, they may feel like asking, "Do you come peaceably?"

The Bethlehemites had ample reason to be afraid. Good things did not always follow when Samuel showed up. His messages were not always very uplifting. Once Samuel had called down thunder and rain at a time when dry weather would have been better for the harvest (1 Samuel 12:17-18). Everyone knew Samuel had spoken a harsh message of rejection to King Saul. If *Samuel* was afraid that Saul might kill him (1 Samuel 16:2), then it's reasonable to imagine the inhabitants of Bethlehem might worry about the same thing. Perhaps they feared getting caught between two powerful forces: Samuel and Saul. For the moment, however, Samuel allayed their fears by telling them that he did in fact come in peace: (1 Samuel 16:5) "I have come to sacrifice to the Lord. Consecrate yourselves, and come with me to the sacrifice." Then he invited Jesse and his sons to the sacrifice.

Verses 6-13—When Samuel sized up Jesse's sons, the oldest—named Eliab—looked like a promising replacement for Saul. The Lord, however, turned Samuel away from making judgments about any of Jesse's sons based on outward appearances. We may wonder what alternative Samuel had. We cannot search anyone else's heart. What else can we use as a basis for judgment other than outward appearances? But the Lord showed Samuel (vv. 7-11) that the one to be anointed king was not yet present.

Verse 11—The Lord's anointed was to be the *youngest* of Jesse's sons. This is entirely in keeping with the Lord's way of doing things. He chooses the foolish, weak, lowly, and despised things to shame the wise and the strong

(1 Corinthians 1:27–28). Thus, a ruddy teenager with a fine appearance and handsome features is anointed with oil in the presence of his brothers, and the Spirit of the Lord came upon him in power (1 Samuel 16:13).

Anointing—the Hebrew word for "one who is anointed" is *meshiach* or, as we have come to say, "Messiah." The Greek word for one who has been anointed is *chrístos* or, as we have come to say, "Christ." David was anointed into God's plan for the ultimate Anointed One. In this sense, he was "Christened."

You have an even better anointing than David had. You were christened in Holy Baptism, probably in the presence of your family, certainly in the power of the Holy Spirit. The Lord comes to common people with things that look common and insignificant. How easily such things can be despised by the world, even as David (17:28) came to be criticized by his oldest brother, Eliab. But through Holy Baptism, the Lord calls us to be His own so that we may live with Him in His kingdom and "serve Him in everlasting righteousness, innocence, and blessedness."

When you feel small and insignificant, you need not despair. You may not just *feel* small—you may actually *be* small when compared to the challenges that face you. But when you take God's Word to heart, how can you help but rejoice greatly in your smallness? When we are small, God is great and can do great things.

2 From Field to Palace (16:14–23)

Verse 14—The Spirit of the Lord departed Saul, and the Lord allowed an evil spirit to torment him. What was this "harmful spirit"? We don't know for sure. It may have been a demon. Or this phrase may be a Hebrew idiom that refers simply to a change in dispositions, which can come and go (e.g., "a case of the blues").

The onset of this "harmful spirit"—the Scripture does not say exactly what it was—provided several opportunities for David to spend time in Saul's court. He came for the first time to this royal court as one who had been anointed king, but who would not take the throne for fifteen years. David came not with sword or crown, but with his harp ("lyre"; v. 16). He came not to rule but to serve. He came in the manner of the Messiah described in Zechariah 4:6—"Not by might, nor by power, but by My Spirit, says the Lord of hosts." Despite the sins Scripture records for David, he never made any attempt to usurp Saul's power or to get or keep any earthly crown. The Spirit of the Lord was with David (v. 18), and Saul was pleased with him (v. 22). Compare Luke 2:52—"And Jesus increased in wisdom and in stature and in favor with God and man."

3 From Sheep-Herder to Giant-Killer (17:1–58)

When David comes up against Goliath, the conflict looks ridiculous. David's youth, his inexperience in battle, and his comparatively small size, however, turn out to be an advantage. They lead him to depend not on himself but on the Lord, who unexpectedly brings about a great salvation through weak and seemingly foolish means.

Some treat the story of David and Goliath as the classic underdog-comes-from-behind-to-win story. But there's more here than meets the eye. Goliath isn't up against a little youth named David. He sees David, but in reality he confronts the Lord God Himself. In this sense, David is no long shot at all, but a sure bet.

David's motives in taking on Goliath may not have been altogether pure. He asks, (v. 26) "What will be done for the man who kills this Philistine and takes away the reproach from Israel?" His oldest brother, Eliab, retorts, (v. 28) "I know your presumption and the evil of your heart." But David's persistence in the matter was reported to Saul, who sends for him. David summarizes his case before Saul, not by calling on self-centered bravado, but rather by saying, (v. 37) "The Lord who delivered me from the paw of the lion and from the paw of the bear will deliver me from the hand of this Philistine."

Verses 38–39—David, who had become one of Saul's armor-bearers (1 Samuel 16:21), then attempted to be one of Saul's armor-wearers. This did not last long. David sheds the unfamiliar military gear and takes up more familiar weapons: his staff and sling. Verse 40 tells us that David picked up five smooth stones. Why five? Did he think he might miss? Perhaps even this was an act of faith, because 2 Samuel 21:18–22 suggests there were four other giants, descendants of Rapha in Gath. If this was the case, and if the accounts of 1 Samuel 17 and 2 Samuel 21 are talking about the same Goliath, then David had one stone for each giant!

Verses 50–54—The contest was short-lived. One stone, probably about the size of a baseball, sank into Goliath's forehead. Goliath's body fell, and his head was soon parted from it (v. 54).

Verses 55–56—As Saul watched David going out to meet the Philistine, he asked Abner, his general, "Whose son is this youth?" It may be that Saul had trouble remembering who David was, since David was probably only one teen among dozens who had come to Saul's court. Then again, the text doesn't say that Saul didn't know who David was, but rather that he asked who his father was. After all, one of the rewards for conquering Goliath was that the victor's family would be exempt from taxes (v. 25). Perhaps Saul asked about David's father so that he could make good on his promised reward.

4 From a King's Favor to a King's Fear (18:1–30)

Verses 1–5—David found a new friend in Saul's son Jonathan, who made a covenant with David because he loved David as much as he loved himself. Jonathan had not inherited his father's fear of losing the throne. Though Jonathan might have claimed his right to succeed his father, he gave up his claim to David in love. David never attempted to treat Jonathan as a subject but always showed him proper respect. After all, the kingship was not a matter of their ability or charisma. This was no political matter but a theological one. It was the work of the Lord.

Verses 6–11—The song of those rejoicing in Israel, however, singled David out as superior to Saul. Saul, who had at first been pleased by David, now became jealous of him. His hand took up a spear, and he tried to pin David to the wall with it. David eluded Saul's attacks twice.

Have you ever seen what happens when an especially gifted young person comes to a club or a workplace and does so well that everyone takes notice? What happens in the hearts and minds of people who have more seniority and more experience when the newcomer outdoes them in every respect? It may be that you have such an "enemy"—or perhaps you know of others who burn with fear and jealousies. Such attitudes must be recognized for what they are: sins, not merely against another person but also against the Lord God Himself, who gifts individuals with abilities. We do better by God's grace to have the heart of a Jonathan than the heart of a Saul.

Conclusion

Only in one other place does the Scripture describe anyone being a person "after [God's] own heart." In Jeremiah 3:15, God says, "And I will give you shepherds after My own heart, who will feed you with knowledge and understanding." Our pastors (the word *pastor* means "shepherd") are to be shepherds after God's own heart. They follow in the path of David, the shepherd anointed to be king. But more important, they serve the Good Shepherd: Jesus, our Lord. By preaching and teaching, they expose the Sauls of this world by proclaiming God's Word in Law. They comfort the Davids by proclaiming God's Gospel of peace and trustworthiness to repentant sinners. God gives us these shepherds that we may ever be comforted, strengthened, guided, and sustained by God through His Word and Sacraments, all throughout our lives that we may be His own, forever.

Concluding Activities

Distribute Study Leaflet 3 as you dismiss the group.

Lecture Leaders Session 3 — Life of David

David on the Run

1 Samuel 19–31

Preparing for the Session

Central Focus

When we suffer unjust attacks, we can endure in patience, waiting for God to act on our behalf. We can rely on His gracious promise never to fail or forsake us.

Objectives

That participants, led by the Holy Spirit working through God's Word, will

1. follow David's movements as he flees from Saul;

2. trust God's care on the basis of the promises in His Word;

3. develop restraint when dealing with adversity; and

4. learn to patiently respect authority, even when those exercising it act in difficult or distressing ways.

Note for the small-group leaders: Lesson notes and other materials you will need begin on page 64.

For the Lecture Leader

This course on the life of David covers a larger portion of Scripture than most other Bible studies of the Life-Light series. As a result, some sections (this unit in particular) include a great deal of factual material. It will not be possible to follow the text in the usual verse-by-verse manner. Rather, we will travel through it, pointing out the most important landmarks along the way.

Among other things, this procedure ought to help participants to realize that we can never exhaust the depths of the Word of God. We will always have more to come back to. Some group members may feel like tourists on a trip to Europe, rushed from site to site without having enough time to take it all in. But remind the class that they can always return to specific Bible portions as they have time. The Holy Spirit is our teacher. He will help us understand and apply those truths He wants to impress on our hearts and imprint on our lives.

It might also be helpful for participants if you display a map while you speak. The map should depict the geography of the time period we are studying—not all of the cities inhabited at the time of David were still in existence at the time of Christ. In some cases, people rebuilt razed cities a short distance away, keeping the same place-name. Perhaps you could enlarge the map from the enrichment magazine.

In addition, you might consult biblical archaeology magazines, encyclopedia, atlases, dictionaries, or the Internet to find pictures of the terrain where David traveled and hid. All of this will help the members of your class get a better picture of what is happening in the texts you lecture about.

Session Plan

Worship

Begin the session with the hymn printed in the study leaflet. Accompaniments are available in denominational hymnals, such as *Lutheran Service Book* or *Lutheran Worship* (refer to hymnal index). (Note: Concordia Publishing House has available *Every Voice a Song,* a nine-CD set of organ accompaniments for 180 hymns and liturgy. All the initial worship hymns in the Life-Light courses are included in this resource. It's especially helpful for mission congregations and small parishes. See the list of study resources on p. 7.) Follow with this prayer:

Prayer

Merciful Lord, You taught Your servant David patience and obedience in the midst of affliction. As You conform us to the image of Your Son through the trials of life, strengthen us by Your Spirit through Your comforting and sustaining Word. In Jesus' name. Amen.

Lecture Presentation

Introduction

It doesn't take much to turn smoldering sin and faithlessness into a blazing wildfire. A little spark of fear can flare into overwhelming anger. The fear of being caught after committing sin, the fear resulting from threats to one's personal pride, the fear of suffering some small injustice, these all too soon develop into a raging firestorm as fear tries to hide behind anger.

We have seen this week how Saul's fears flared to become a terrible rage. What had been episodic outbursts now became an endless obsession. The downward spiral continues until, finally, Saul's self-destruction is complete. Let's review how and why that happened.

1 Saul Would Spear David (19:1–23:29)

In 1 Samuel 19:6, Saul took an oath: "As the LORD lives, he [David] shall not be put to death." Indeed, the living Lord did not allow David to be put to death, but that did not stop Saul from trying, despite his oath. Soon after the oath (19:8–17), Saul tried to pin David to a wall with a spear—for the second time. When that failed, he had some of his more unscrupulous men watch David's house, with an eye toward assassination. Saul's daughter Michal, now David's wife, helped him escape through a window (cf. Joshua 2:15 and Acts 9:25).

19:18—Saul's pursuit then began in earnest. King Saul's energies and resources should have been spent on the Philistines, Israel's enemies. But Saul was intent on pursuing David. Where would you go first if someone were trying to kill you? David fled first to Samuel, the prophet who had anointed him. He knew he would not find in Samuel a military or political ally. He did not intend to mount a force to depose Saul. Instead, he sought the wisdom and comfort of the Lord's Word. Perhaps you have known the words of a mother, father, or friend who encouraged you when you were afraid or in trouble. How comforting it can be to hear the Word of the Lord from those who know and love Him too.

19:20–24—Ironically, the words of the Lord from the mouths of Saul's own men—and from Saul's own mouth—prevented them from harming David. As we see this, we can't help but recall that one day all enemies of Christ and His people will be rendered powerless by His Word. In that day (Philippians 2:10–11), *every* knee will bow and *every* tongue will confess that Jesus Christ is Lord to the glory of God the Father!

20:1–42—After meeting with Samuel, David next went to his friend Jonathan. (V. 1) "What have I done?" David asks. In verse 32, Jonathan asked his father that same question, "What has he done?" Saul gives no answer (v. 33), but instead treats Jonathan as if he were David, hurling his spear at his own son!

Like David, we usually seek logical, rational connections and explanations for the pain and heartache we suffer. We ask why. But sometimes there are no rational answers. Sometimes we must simply admit to ourselves that we live in a fallen world, a world in which Satan and the misery sin brings affect us all—believers and unbelievers alike. And yet our Lord does not leave us comfortless. Often He graciously provides friends like Jonathan who will stand by us, who will speak the Word of God to us. To whom can you be a friend like that this week? To whom can you speak the Gospel of Christ's love and forgiveness even in times of great trouble and fear?

21:1–9—David, who at first had fled to Samuel at Ramah, and then to his friend Jonathan, went next to Ahimelech—the priest at Nob. As David speaks (vv. 2–3), we see the continuation of a trend. David has become used to deception. In 19:12–13, Michal, David's wife, had deceived her father in order to help David escape. In 20:28–29, Jonathan had lied to Saul about David's actions and whereabouts. Now David practiced such deception himself. His lies persuaded the priest to do a very unusual thing. The bread of the Presence was set aside by the Lord for use only by the priests. Ordinary Israelites were not supposed to eat it; it was holy (Leviticus 24:9). But Ahimelech (v. 6) gave the consecrated bread to David anyway, rationalizing that if David and his men were on a holy mission, then he and his men might partake of the holy bread.

Most of us view the idea of lying to a priest with consternation. But we note that this incident becomes one more link in God's plan of salvation. In Matthew 12:1–4, our Lord Jesus Christ used these facts to thwart the Pharisees and their legalism. God can use anything—even the sins of His people—to accomplish His purposes. We do not, of course, justify our sins in this way. We surely do not accuse God of condoning sin or—heaven forbid—of causing it. Yet Romans 8:28 shows us that God works *all things* together for good for those who love Him. As we yield our lives to Him—yes, even the evil we see in those lives—we can trust Him to work in us a deeper horror at the thought of offending Him and a deeper appreciation for His enormous mercy and grace.

21:10–15—We easily understand David's visit to a prophet, a friend, and a priest. But David's next trip took him to an *enemy*—Achish, king of Gath. Gath, you remember, was Goliath's hometown!

Remember the song (1 Samuel 18:7) "Saul has struck down his thousands, and David his ten thousands"? This song had ignited the first spark of fear and jealousy in Saul. Now the people of Gath remembered the lyrics too! The servants of King Achish reminded him of it (21:11). David probably wished that the song had never been composed! It followed him wherever he went, whether he liked it or not. David resorted to yet another deception, that of madness, in order to make his escape (vv. 12–15).

Now (22:1) David headed for a solitary place—the cave of Adullam. It did not remain a lonely place for long. Word got out to his family and friends—and (v. 2) to everyone who was in distress or in debt or discontented. To his credit, David could have incited this band of about four hundred malcontents against Saul, but he never did. Would you have been equally restrained?

22:3–10—David apparently would have been satisfied to find a safe haven for his family in Moab and perhaps a safe haven for himself in (v. 4) Moab's stronghold, but the prophet Gad (v. 5) told him to go back into Judah. Meanwhile (vv. 6–10), Saul was back on David's trail thanks to Doeg the Edomite. Saul had shown contempt for priests before. This time his contempt was to become murder.

22:11–23—Enraged by what he saw as treason (v. 17), Saul nevertheless could not bring himself to kill the priests. He ordered his guards to do it. They refused. So Saul turned to (v. 18) Doeg the Edomite, who killed eighty-five priests that day and then (v. 19) turned to massacre the men and women of Nob, their children and infants, cattle, donkeys, and sheep. A son of Ahimelech, Abiathar, survived. David, probably regretting his earlier deception of Ahimelech, felt responsible for all these sad events (vv. 22–23); he offered Abiathar protection. Years later, this loyal follower would help to preserve David's life.

23:1–12—As we have noted, King Saul ought to have been fighting the Philistines instead of chasing David. How interesting, then, that David—the one who is being chased by Saul—is the one who protected God's people, doing what Saul should have done.

David rescued the people of Keilah from the Philistines. Even so (vv. 11–12), they were all too ready to surrender David and his men to Saul. Have you ever made sacrifices for people who didn't appreciate what you had done? So, too, our Lord Jesus Christ came to rescue His people—and those same people were all too ready to betray Him and to surrender Him to His executioners. We need not seethe in anger when this happens. Instead, we can entrust ourselves to our Savior-God, our faithful Creator. He knows our motives—and those of our enemies. He forgives our sins. And He will see to our ultimate reward.

23:13–29—By this time (v. 13), about six hundred men had joined David's ragtag army. Finding food and safe places to camp must have become more and more difficult. Then (v. 19) the inhabitants of Ziph told Saul where to find David. But before Saul could capitalize on the information he received from the Ziphite informants (vv. 26–29), the Lord allowed Israel's perennial enemies, the Philistines, to take the heat off David. The Lord knows how to save us—even at the last moment—using the most unlikely sources!

2 David Would Spare Saul (24:1–27:12)

24:1–15—The Philistines didn't keep Saul busy for long. Someone gave Saul David's location once again (perhaps the Ziphites were still trailing David). Countless caves and crags dot the terrain in Israel. But Saul (v. 3) chose to relieve himself in the very same cave where David was hiding. (V. 4) Saul couldn't have been any more vulnerable than at that moment. Nevertheless, David had such respect for the position Saul held under God that he was conscience-stricken for having cut the hem off Saul's royal robe (vv. 5–7). David regretted having possibly humiliated the king. He forbade his men to harm Saul. What a rare thing to find such a respect for authority—then and now!

24:16–20—Saul had shown incomplete repentance so often that David could no longer be fooled into trusting him. Respecting the position Saul held and trusting Saul himself were two different things. Saul (vv. 21–22) wanted David to swear not to harm Saul's descendants. David easily took that oath, because he had made it earlier to Jonathan. And yet (v. 22), David headed back to his stronghold instead of remaining in Saul's service. He knew better than to entrust himself to Saul.

26:1–25—Not long after, David spared Saul's life the second time. David did not wait for Saul to come to him. Instead, he slipped into the heart of Saul's camp while Saul's army slept. David took Abishai, one of his nephews, with him. As before, Saul could not have been more helpless. But once again, David showed the utmost respect for King Saul, "the LORD's anointed." This time, however, David got *his* hand on Saul's spear—perhaps the same spear Saul had repeatedly hurled at him. When David confronted Saul this time (v. 21), Saul vowed not to try to harm David anymore. He apparently kept his word; from this moment until the report of Saul's death, we read of no more such attempts on David's life.

27:1–12—David nonetheless still feared Saul and his schemes. And so (vv. 1–3) David once again returned to the Philistines, asking for what amounted to political asylum. He had once played the madman in Philistia. This time he played on King Achish's gullibility. Because David had become so odious to Saul (v. 12), Achish was willing to believe David would be a faithful servant of Philistia. But instead, Achish's trust gave David the opportunity to use deception once again. In verses 8–11, David led Achish to believe he (David) was raiding Israelite towns, when in fact David and his men were annihilating Israel's enemies to the southwest. But David (v. 11) prudently left no survivors who could testify against him in Philistia.

3 From Spear to Spiritist (28:1–25)

As 1 Samuel ends, we see Saul go from bad to worse. Having been afflicted by evil spirits from whom he sought relief, he now decided to contact the dead through a medium (witch) of Endor! This was the worst kind of occult practice. The Lord had forbidden it in no uncertain terms. Just exactly what happened in Endor remains something of a mystery. Some have thought the medium did contact Samuel. In that case, God allowed it in a unique situation to accomplish His own purposes for Israel and David. More likely, the medium conjured up an evil spirit who took the form of Samuel. Note that she described (v. 14) it in only these generic words: "An old man . . . wrapped in a robe." Saul, who had come looking for Samuel, believed it to be Samuel. Whatever or whoever it was frightened the medium. It ignored her and began to converse with Saul. It began to accuse Saul of all his wrongdoings (vv. 17–19). Satan's very name in Hebrew means "the accuser"!

Evil spirits know very well what goes on here on earth. They are able to capitalize on this knowledge. If this was a demon, it turned Saul away from hope in God's forgiveness to despair at the coming judgment. Saul fell full length to the ground (v. 20), overwhelmed by the fears that had plagued him since the day David killed Goliath. How ironic (v. 24) that a medium—one who trafficked with demons—prepared Saul's last supper.

4 From Spear to Arrow to Sword (29:1–31:13)

29:1–11—Meanwhile, David continued his ruse, raiding and pillaging nomadic tribes. The other Philistine leaders (v. 3) were not as gullible as King Achish. They insisted that Achish leave David at home (vv. 4–5) as they reminded Achish of David's victory song: "Saul has struck down his thousands, and David his ten thousands." In verse 7, Achish reluctantly turned David away, and (v. 8) David maintained his front by objecting to Achish's decision. Thus, God spared David from fighting his own people, from any future accusations of treason and from taking part in the battle in which Saul would be killed. God did for David what David could not do for himself, sparing David from some of the consequences of his faithless folly in trying to find refuge among Israel's enemies.

As 1 Samuel 30 opens, David has returned to his Ziklag base camp. There he found that he and his men had gotten a dose of their own medicine. The Amalekites had raided and pillaged his stronghold; they had not massacred the women and children as David himself had been doing to his enemies but had instead kidnapped them. David's men were so grieved that they considered stoning him, "But David found strength in the Lord his God" (v. 6 NIV). How we need to remember to do that too, especially in life's hardest, most threatening times; when even our trusted friends seem to turn against us, the Lord will never abandon us.

30:7–8—Even in this seeming disaster, though, the Lord was at work. The trouble moved David even farther from the battle in which Saul and Jonathan would be killed. Instead of fighting either the Philistines or Saul, David and his army chased the Amalekites. The Lord preserved for David and his men everything the Amalekites had taken (30:18–19).

31:1–6—The Philistines gained great victory over Saul that day. Wounded by Philistine archers, Saul now faced his own death (v. 4). He was in the habit of getting others to do his killing for him (except when he was in a rage); now he asked his armor-bearer to help him commit suicide. But the armor-bearer refused; so (31:5) Saul fell on his own sword. The armor-bearer then fell on his sword too.

31:8–10—Saul's fears about being abused were realized despite his attempts to prevent it. The Philistines cut off his head, stripped him of his armor, and fastened his body to the wall of Beth Shan. At a later date (2 Samuel 21:12–14), David had the bones of Saul and Jonathan brought home for a decent burial.

Conclusion

Fear and its cousin jealousy can inflame our soul. What

do you do when you are angry? Are you tempted to enlist others to join your cause, to help you avenge the wrong you have endured?

Saul's fear never abated, and his anger was never satisfied. In the end, it completely consumed him. Perhaps David learned from watching Saul's foolishness. Listen to David's words from Psalm 4:4–5: "Be angry, and do not sin; ponder in your own hearts on your beds, and be silent. Offer right sacrifices, and put your trust in the Lord." Note that here God does not forbid anger. Rather, He urges us not to sin in our anger. Perhaps we, like Saul, let ourselves become terribly jealous. Perhaps we let ourselves be drawn into rash acts or heated words. Saul's life warns us of the dangers posed by anger and fear.

But Saul's life is more than just a warning. Here God would speak to our hearts, reminding us that His work in us and not our own determined resolve will enable us to live lives that do not surrender to the pressures of fear and anger. It is the work of our Lord Jesus Christ to breathe new life into us through His Word of pardon and peace. He forgives our failures, and in His Word and Sacraments He empowers us to live free from the bondage fear and anger can cause in our lives. No matter the difficulties we may be facing, we may recall that our gracious Lord has promised never to fail or forsake us but to preserve and sustain us always, and even eternally.

Concluding Activities

Distribute Study Leaflet 4 as you dismiss the group.

Lecture Leaders Session 4 — **Life of David**

David on the Rise

2 Samuel 1:1–5:5

Preparing for the Session

Central Focus

David resisted shedding the blood of Saul and his kinsmen. Despite this, war breaks out between those in Israel loyal to Saul and those in Judah loyal to David. Nevertheless, David unites the two kingdoms with wisdom and justice.

Objectives

That participants, led by the Holy Spirit working through God's Word, will

1. see how David, the Lord's anointed, is acknowledged as king by Israel and Judah;

2. identify the rivalries in their own lives that could easily escalate into open conflict; and

3. pursue peace and godliness.

Note for the small-group leaders: Lesson notes and other materials you will need begin on page 68.

For the Lecture Leader

Session Plan

Worship

Begin the session with the hymn printed in the study leaflet. Accompaniments are available in denominational hymnals, such as *Lutheran Service Book* or *Lutheran Worship* (refer to hymnal index). (Note: Concordia Publishing House has available *Every Voice a Song*, a nine-CD set of organ accompaniments for 180 hymns and liturgy. All the initial worship hymns in the Life-Light courses are included in this resource. It's especially helpful for mission congregations and small parishes. See the list of study resources on p. 7.) Follow with this prayer:

Prayer

Lord Jesus Christ, You give us Your peace, the peace that passes all understanding. When we face conflict and trouble in our lives, cause us to repent, trusting in Your boundless mercy, and enable us to bring Your peace to others who need it. We ask this in Your name. Amen.

Lecture Presentation

Introduction

Have you ever been elected to serve on a church board or as an officer in some other organization? Were you elected because no one else wanted to serve or did you have to run against someone whom you considered a friend?

David was elected by one vote: the Lord's vote. David had not volunteered to serve as Israel's king, nor had he pursued it with whatever political influence or military might he could have mustered. For all we know, he would have been satisfied to go back to the fields as a shepherd or to serve the king's court as a psalmist or an army officer, two things he did well.

God had elected David king by His own will. All the wrangling of human beings could not stop God's purposes in David's life. While the Lord's favor encouraged David, human behavior grieved him. David ascended to the throne only after seeing the depth of human envy and depravity.

1 David, Rising from the Depths of Grief (1:1–27)

As we have seen in an earlier session, Saul had set David up to die at the hand of the Philistines. But as this week's Scriptures have shown, Saul himself was the one to be mortally wounded in battle with these uncircumcised pagans. David's words to Abishai came true, (1 Samuel 26:9–10) "Who can put out his hand against the LORD's anointed and be guiltless?" And David said, "As the LORD lives, the LORD will strike him, or his day will come to die, or he will go down into battle and perish."

It was particularly ironic that an Amalekite brought the

news to David. The Lord had previously commanded Saul to annihilate the Amalekites (1 Samuel 14:48; 15:2–3; 28:18), not sparing a single man, woman, infant, or child. Not even the Amalekite cattle and sheep, camels, or donkeys were to be allowed to live. Saul failed to obey. Now an Amalekite carried the news of Saul's demise to the future king of God's people, David.

Verses 1–16—David, however, took no pleasure in this news. The details related by the Amalekite in verses 4–10 differ from those in 1 Samuel 31:2–6. The Amalekite certainly had to have been in a hurry to have traveled (vv. 1, 6) the distance from Mount Gilboa to Ziklag—possibly close to 100 miles—over rough terrain in three days. Perhaps he wanted to tell his version and steal off with a reward before the facts about Saul's death became known to David.

The Amalekite had Saul's crown and arm band to corroborate his story. David did not quibble about the details. He was dismayed at the Amalekite's delight at having had a hand in the death of the "Lord's anointed." David's respect for the Lord and for the servants of the Lord is the same kind of respect God wants us to have for one another. This includes especially those who have been installed into the pastoral office, instituted and ordained to dispense the life-giving Means of Grace. But it also extends to all those who live in Christ, the Messiah, the Anointed One. We honor and esteem one another in the Body of Christ, not on the basis of how pious or how charming each person may be but rather because each of us is "the Lord's anointed one" in Jesus Christ through Holy Baptism. Those enemies of the cross who injure or harm us, the "Lord's anointed," will bear their own guilt. They will have to answer to the Lord, who by grace has christened us poor sinners as His own dear children.

Verses 16–27—The Amalekite's own words testified against him. David occupied the mouths of his supporters with something more constructive. He ordered the men of Judah to be taught "The Lament of the Bow." In doing so, David kept them from saying anything less-than-kind about Saul. The words of this song were (v. 18) also recorded in the book of Jashar—literally, "the book of the upright," a poetic history of the deeds of heroic Israelites. This book has been lost in antiquity.

People for generations have encouraged one another to "speak nothing but good about the dead." David's lament says only good things about Saul and Jonathan. While (vv. 24–26) the daughters of Israel wept for Saul, David grieved for Jonathan, whom he called his "brother," and whose love was "surpassing the love of women."

The word *eulogy* literally means "a good word." It is a common practice at death for a loved one to give a eulogy, to speak some good words about the person who has died. The best time for this, however, may not be in the funeral service itself, because we want nothing to suggest that anyone's good works merit God's favor. We want nothing to obscure the fact that our comfort comes always and only through the righteous work of Jesus Christ.

2 David, Rising to Be King over Judah (2:1–7)

In the course of time, David's grief subsided. For whatever reason, David decided it was time to move. When he inquired of the Lord, the Lord directed him and his army to Hebron.

Saul had made his home and capital at Gibeah, to the north of Jerusalem (1 Samuel 10:5; 15:34). Hebron was a town in Judah. There, David was publicly anointed as king of Judah. It would be (v. 11) another seven and a half years before all twelve tribes would unite under David's rule.

3 Israel Rises Up against Judah (2:8–4:12)

Before we go on, it would be good to review the term *Israel*. Students of the Scriptures soon learn that certain words have more than one meaning. The term *Israel* is one such word. This name was first given to the patriarch Jacob (Genesis 32:22–32) after he wrestled with God as he returned home from exile. Later, the term *Israel* applied to Jacob's descendants. Sometimes the term refers to a geographical area, and sometimes it refers only to the ten tribes that settled in the northern part of Canaan, the Northern Kingdom. It can even be applied to those who are not of the Hebrew race at all, but who are heirs of God by faith in Christ. (See Romans 9:6b: "For not all who are descended from Israel belong to Israel.")

For our purposes here today, the term *Israel* will refer to the northern tribes, as distinguished from *Judah*, the southern tribes, who were descended from the tribe of Judah and settled in southern Canaan. The smaller tribe of Benjamin is included in the term *Judah* also. In Joshua 11:21, the Bible first distinguishes between Israel and Judah. After the death of Solomon, the split between Israel and Judah—that is, between the northern and southern tribes—became all the more pronounced.

David's rise to power over a united Israel was not uncontested. One of Saul's surviving sons, Ish-bosheth, ten years David's elder (see 2 Samuel 2:10; 5:4), was commandeered and appointed king by Saul's general, Abner. The tension caused by this divided kingdom came to a head when Abner and his men met David's general, Joab, and his men at the pool of Gibeon.

2:14-17—Sometimes the most bitter feuds are kindled between the closest family members. The most deep-seated resentment can set in between members of the same family. What apparently began (v. 14) as some sort of a contest ended up (v. 16) in a fierce melee. The children of God were no longer doing battle against their ungodly neighbors; they were fighting among themselves, killing each other! (See v. 26.)

2:18-23—As David's men began to chase off the men of Israel, Saul's general, Abner, was hotly pursued by one of David's nephews, Asahel. Asahel was a brother of Abishai, the soldier who had gone with David into Saul's camp (1 Samuel 26:6-12). Joab, Asahel's other brother, was—as you know—David's general. Asahel was (v. 18) "as swift of foot as a wild gazelle," but he was no match for Abner's strength. Abner warned Asahel to stop chasing him, and when Asahel persisted (vv. 22-23), Abner ran the blunt end of his spear through Asahel's stomach and out his back. Perhaps Abner did not realize his own strength. It's entirely possible the grisly death was accidental. It certainly stunned all who heard about it.

2:26-32—Again, Abner called for an end to the hostilities. Joab agreed, and each group went its separate way—but Joab would get his revenge. Nineteen of David's men had died, but 360 Benjamites lost their lives. Because of this incident, (3:1) "there was a long war between the house of Saul and the house of David."

3:6-11—During this war, Abner strengthened his own position in the courts of Ish-bosheth. As Ish-bosheth sensed his own power wane, he began to suffer the kind of paranoia that often afflicts insecure rulers, the kind of paranoia that tormented Saul. He made a rash accusation against Abner, who in turn became deeply offended. He abandoned Ish-bosheth and turned his allegiance—as well as that of Israel's elders—toward David.

3:12-27—Joab, still bitter that Abner had killed Joab's brother, suspected that Abner's newfound loyalty to David was a trick. He couldn't believe that David would accept Abner's offer of peace. Perhaps Joab also felt jealous at the thought that Abner might draw away some of Joab's influence and power as David's military commander. And so (vv. 26-27), Joab avenged his brother's death. He stabbed an unsuspecting Abner in the stomach.

3:28-39—David's reproach of Joab's ruthless deed and his heartfelt lament at the death of Abner gained the respect of all Israel's people. Everyone knew that David had not plotted Abner's murder, nor had he approved it. David commanded that Joab tear his clothes, put on sackcloth, and walk in mourning in front of Abner's funeral procession. This order caused a rift between David and Joab that would never heal. In some of his last words before he died, David asked his son Solomon to bring Joab to justice: (1 Kings 2:5-6) "Do not let his [Joab's] gray head go down to [the grave] in peace." Why didn't David enforce justice himself? We don't know. A case can be made that he should have.

4:1-12—The bloodshed continued. Two hotheads among Saul's former troops decided to finish the unification of Israel Abner had begun. These men, Rechab and Baanah, slipped into Ish-bosheth's house and (vv. 5-6) stabbed him while he lay taking his noonday rest. They thought to curry David's favor by bringing Ish-bosheth's head to David, but instead (vv. 9-12) they provoked his wrath for their cowardly, disloyal act. Like the Amalekite who thought he was bringing good news to David at the death of Saul, these men (v. 12) were executed at David's command. Their hands and feet were cut off and their bodies hung in public display, as was customary in the ancient world. The display warned all would-be traitors to think before they rebelled against God and their rulers. How gruesome life had become for that gentle shepherd boy who once roamed the hills around Bethlehem!

4 David, Rising to Be King over All Israel (5:1-5)

Abner's diplomacy was not in vain. All Israel had come to look to David for leadership. Ironically, this happened as Abner's lifeless body lay in the same tomb with Ish-bosheth's head (v. 12)! All the tribes of Israel came to Hebron, as had Abner before them. They acknowledged, (v. 1) "We are your bone and flesh," even as they confessed the Word of the Lord, (v. 2) "You shall be shepherd of My people Israel, and you shall be prince over Israel."

All the elders of Israel (v. 3) anointed David king. David would reign over all Israel and Judah (v. 5) for thirty-three years, the same number of years that his Greater Son, Jesus Christ, would live before He was crucified. This Shepherd King would be established forever.

Conclusion

Human history testifies that the rise and fall of rulers is

often bloody. The Scriptures confirm this. But the Bible has not a hopeless intent but a hopeful one. By it, our Lord wants to show our desperate need for salvation, which He Himself has brought about in our Lord Jesus.

We can say in all fairness that David's rise to reign over Judah and Israel was bathed in blood, though little of it to this point was shed by David's choice. The rise of our Lord Jesus Christ to reign over His kingdom of grace was every bit as grisly as anything we have read thus far. Death by crucifixion was horrendous. Such a death would have ended the reign of any mere mortal ruler. But for Jesus Christ, true God and true man, being lifted up on the cross marked the beginning of His eternal reign as our King of grace.

How easy it would be for us to shake our heads with contempt at the terrible things we have read about in the life of David. How easy it would be for us to imagine ourselves as much more civilized or morally innocent than Israel's citizens back then. We imagine ourselves innocent of the lust for power and incapable of the violence we have seen in David and in those around him. But when we consider our hearts in the clear light of God's Law, we see that our sins are every bit as wretched as the sins of those about whom we are reading. We, too, fail to love. We, too, thirst for power. We, too, hold grudges and look for ways to get even with those who slight or insult or hurt us.

Thanks be to God that He has given us a Savior who was bloodied for our sakes and who empowers us to rise above our grudges, vengefulness, and lust for power. Thank God for the Savior who has become our King of grace so that we may live under Him and serve Him in everlasting righteousness, innocence, and blessedness!

Concluding Activities

Close with a prayer that flows from the words of Psalm 28:8—"The Lord is the strength of His people; He is the saving refuge of His anointed."

Then distribute Study Leaflet 5 as you dismiss the group.

Lecture Leaders Session 5 — Life of David

David on the Throne

2 Samuel 5:6–10:19

Preparing for the Session

Central Focus

David consolidates the kingdom and conquers neighboring enemies. In one case, he overpowers a mighty stronghold called Jerusalem and makes it his capital. He plans to build a temple for the Lord, but the Lord promises something better: an eternal dynasty for David's Greater Son.

Objectives

That participants, led by the Holy Spirit working through God's Word, will

1. recognize David's God-given political, military, and diplomatic skills in building the nation of Israel;

2. review God's promise to David and its fulfillment in Christ; and

3. rely more fully on God's promises in their Baptism.

Note for the small-group leaders: Lesson notes and other materials you will need begin on page 71.

For the Lecture Leader

A Bible dictionary, a Bible atlas, and a concordance will come in handy for this session. Use the Bible atlas to locate the places you read about. Note the direction of those places, north, east, west, and south, in relation to Jerusalem. Are the areas in rough terrain or green valleys? Compare the distances between places with the distances between your city and other cities around you. You might even use a photocopier to enlarge or reduce images. Make a map of your state that matches the scale of a map of Israel. Place the maps side by side, or make overhead transparencies to give people a better idea of the relative distances involved.

You can use a biblical dictionary and concordance to learn a little bit more about the background of the people and places you read about in the text. A computerized Bible-search program would be especially helpful. If you dig deeply enough, you will find some interesting connections in the past or future history of Israel to shed further light on the events in 2 Samuel and their meanings. A Bible dictionary also will help you with pronunciations.

Many names—both of people and places—in this section are difficult to pronounce. Tell your group this, and pronounce a few of these names so that the members of your group will feel less intimidated during their small-group discussions. Urge participants who have study Bibles to use the notes and cross references in them: sometimes the meaning of a name is given; these meanings are often significant. Encourage the participants to pay particular attention to the double entendres. They often contain truths that might not otherwise be apparent.

Session Plan

Worship

Begin the session with the hymn printed in the study leaflet. Accompaniments are available in denominational hymnals, such as *Lutheran Service Book* or *Lutheran Worship* (refer to hymnal index). (Note: Concordia Publishing House has available *Every Voice a Song*, a nine-CD set of organ accompaniments for 180 hymns and liturgy. All the initial worship hymns in the Life-Light courses are included in this resource. It's especially helpful for mission congregations and small parishes. See the list of study resources on p. 7.) Follow with this prayer:

Prayer

Lord God, You gave Your servant David skills in establishing government according to Your will. Bless our elected and appointed leaders, Lord, so that filled with wisdom and justice, they make and administer laws for the good of all people. We ask this through Christ, our Lord. Amen.

Lecture Presentation

Introduction

Did you have much choice in choosing the town or city in which you live? Would you choose a different site for your home or business if you could?

In this unit, we find David ready to settle down after years on the run. His hometown was Bethlehem, but he had lived in Gath and Ziklag and Hebron—when he wasn't living in a cave or in the wilderness. Having been anointed and acclaimed as king over both Judah and Israel, he begins to look for a suitable capital. He could have chosen to remain in Hebron, but that may have seemed as though he was favoring Judah. He might have taken over Saul's or Ish-bosheth's courts in Gibeah or Gibeon, but that may have seemed as though he was favoring Israel. Instead, he chose a place where North and South meet, where Israel and Judah came together. He set his face toward Jerusalem, the reputedly impenetrable stronghold of the Jebusites.

1 A New City for David (5:6–25)

David could have chosen a capital city that would have been much easier to conquer. Jerusalem at the time was not as large as one of today's super-stores—Walmart or Home Depot. Jerusalem was, however, a natural fortress because of the steep cliffs that led up to its walls on three sides.

The Israelites had overcome the city briefly once before—as they made their way into the Promised Land—but they did not hold this fortress for long. From Joshua 15:63 and Judges 1:21, we learn that the Jebusites quickly recovered it. Prior to David, the Israelites had never quite managed to rid the Promised Land of numerous pockets of resistance, foreigners entrenched in difficult-to-reach places. David was to put an end to that.

Verses 6–7—The Jebusites were so sure of themselves that they boasted to David, "You will not come in here, but the blind and the lame will ward you off." In short order, however, David captured "the stronghold of Zion, that is, the City of David" (cf. 1 Chronicles 11:4–8). Some forty-five times, the Old Testament calls Jerusalem the "City of David"; forty-two of these occur in the books of Samuel, Kings, and Chronicles.

In the centuries after David, the stronghold of Jerusalem would be conquered many times. But the most notable of all victories was won by a King who did not come by force. Jesus, the Son of David, entered the city in humbleness and love. He conquered the hearts of many, winning them by the grace of God.

Verse 10—"David became greater and greater, for the LORD, the God of hosts, was with him." This is significant in many ways, foremost because David was a shadow, a type, a picture of Jesus Christ, who is Himself Immanuel—God with us (Matthew 1:23). We today share a victory greater than what David enjoyed. God is really with us, too, in Christ. He touches us in His Word, in Holy Baptism, and in the bread and wine of Holy Communion. In Christ, we have triumphed over the powers of sin, Satan, and even death. These cannot enslave us, because of what our Savior has done. The Lord God Almighty is with us too, even as He was with David. In that confidence, pastor and people speak the words of the liturgy: "The Lord be with you. And also with you."

Not all foreign powers in David's day were hostile to the kingdoms of Judah and Israel. Outside the boundaries of the Promised Land lived Hiram of Tyre. Archaeological evidence suggests that Hiram took notice of David because of some mutual needs. Hiram's kingdom consisted of lands that were not very agriculturally productive. Hiram did, however, have technical skills and raw materials that Israel did not (cf. 1 Kings 5:10–11; 1 Chronicles 14:1; 2 Chronicles 2:16). Hiram would also have wanted access to the trade routes that David controlled. Solomon, David's successor on Israel's throne, called on Hiram for help in building the temple.

Verse 12—"And David knew that the LORD had established him king over Israel, and that He had exalted His kingdom for the sake of His people Israel." David was fully aware that the successes he had seen did not come on account of some personal quality in himself. He knew that the Lord blessed His people for His own sake. David reflected this truth in his psalms (cf. Psalm 23:3; 25:11; 31:3; 109:21; and 143:11). The danger for David—and the danger for us—is in narrowing our concerns to our own personal and petty wishes instead of seeing our lives as a part of the big picture of the Lord's purpose, the Lord's kingdom. In prospering David, God was preparing a people among whom the Savior would one day be born. In blessing us, God is at work that we might witness His grace and glory in Christ Jesus to the ends of the earth.

Verses 17–25—In contrast to Hiram's Phoenician kingdom, the Philistines could not have been happy to hear that Israel and Judah had been united under David. Can you imagine the look on King Achish's face at this news? Consider, too, what the Philistines must have thought when they again heard the name of David—David who had defeated Goliath! But having overwhelmed Saul, the Philistines probably imagined that they could put a stop to David as well. (V. 17) "All the Philistines went up to search for David," but they had no better luck finding David than had Saul. (Vv. 19–20) Now, however, instead of being on the run as he had been from Saul, David struck out on the offensive against the Philistines as directed by the Lord.

The Philistines abandoned their idols (v. 21) as they ran from the destruction of the Lord. David and his men carried the idols off and (v. 25) struck down the Philistines all the way from Geba to Gezer.

2 A New Place for the Ark (6:1–23)

Verses 1–4—Baale-judah, also known as Kiriath-jearim, lay in the territory between Geba and Gezer. It had been controlled by the Philistines. The ark of the covenant, (v. 2) "which is called by the name of the LORD of hosts who sits enthroned on the cherubim," had been at Baale-judah for several decades. Previously, Israel had kept the ark in the tabernacle at Gibeon. It belonged in the tabernacle. But during the period of the judges (before King Saul), the Israelite army foolishly attempted to use it as a good luck charm in battle against the Philistines. The Philistines had captured it, thinking they had scored a great coup. But one of the main lessons the Lord had attempted to teach people of Old Testament times was this: *When the holy meets what is unholy, the unholy is destroyed.* When the Philistines stole the holy ark of the covenant, they quickly learned this lesson. You can read the account of how and why they returned the ark to Israel in 1 Samuel 5–7.

Solomon would be the one to return the other sacred objects from the tabernacle at Gibeon to the temple in Jerusalem when he had built it. For the time being, however, when David passed through Baale-judah, victorious over the Philistines, it seemed to him a great opportunity to place the ark in his new capital, Jerusalem.

Verse 5—Everybody celebrated as the ark of God was moved toward Jerusalem (v. 3) on a new cart. But when the oxen stumbled (vv. 6–7), it looked like the ark would tip off the cart. Uzzah stretched out his hand to steady it—and the Lord struck Uzzah down for this "error." Perhaps this seems harsh to you. Was God unjust?

Verse 8—David apparently thought so. He became instantly furious. But the Lord had clearly told His people how to transport the ark in Numbers 4:15: "And when Aaron and his sons have finished covering the sanctuary and all the furnishings of the sanctuary, as the camp sets out, after that the sons of Kohath shall come to carry these, but they must not touch the holy things, lest they die." These instructions say nothing about a cart. The Kohathites, descendants of Aaron, were to carry it on long poles. These poles ran through rings attached to the ark so no one would have to touch the holy ark, God's throne on earth.

Everyone in Israel knew the procedure the Lord had commanded. Uzzah was guilty. But as leader and king, so was David himself. And so were the priests. They had treated the holiest symbol of God's presence among them like something common, something unholy.

Verses 8–9—David exploded in anger. Perhaps he was angry at himself for his lack of leadership, a lapse that led to the death of one of his men. Perhaps he was angry with God for being so exacting, so "picky." After all, they were trying to worship. They were doing their best.

Then as now, human beings are reluctant to admit that "our best" isn't good enough. Sin and sinners are destroyed by holiness. That's not harsh; it's the reality of holiness. When someone plummets down the face of a 500-foot cliff, gravity isn't being harsh or cruel—gravity is just a reality. So with holiness. God's people—those who were to enjoy His presence in worship, those who were to represent Him on earth to the nations, those who were to be the nation that would cradle the world's Messiah—needed to know and respect the power of holiness. When the reality of this hit David (v. 9), his anger turned to fear.

The anger we sometimes feel at God's seeming unfairness turns to fear as easily as did David's when we realize that God's wrath could just as easily strike out at us at any moment. We, too, are sinners who have offended a holy God. Where the Law of the Lord is forgotten or trivialized, holiness becomes deadly. But where the Law of the Lord is fulfilled, as it is in Jesus Christ, holiness bears every blessing. In this light, we must regard as truly awesome the fact that poor miserable sinners touch, take, and eat the holy body and blood of Jesus Christ in the Lord's Supper! Holy Communion brings either great blessing or great condemnation. Condemnation occurs where God's Word is downplayed by those who stand in judgment of it; blessing comes to those who know they stand judged and examined under every word of God's Law and who cling to Jesus in repentance and faith.

Verses 10–11—David had felt such fear in the wake of

God's wrath that he changed his mind about bringing the ark into Jerusalem. He left it at the house of a Levite named Obed-edom, since Levites were supposed to know how properly to handle the ark of the covenant.

Verses 12–14—But when David saw the blessings that came to the house of Obed-edom because of the ark, his joy returned, and he changed his mind again. All Israel brought the ark into their new capital. David (v. 14) "danced before the Lord with all his might" in worship.

Verses 14–23—David's first wife, Michal, looked upon this behavior with disdain. It's important to note (v. 14) that David had taken off his royal robes. He wasn't naked, but he was dressed like a "commoner," like an ordinary citizen of Israel, as just one of God's people. Michal did not think this becoming of royalty—something she had known all her life as the daughter of Saul. But David responded, (v. 22) "I will make myself yet more contemptible than this, and I will be abased in your eyes. But by the female servants of whom you have spoken, by them I shall be held in honor." The incident estranged the couple; (v. 23) David apparently avoided marital relations with Michal from that day on.

When viewed in the context of God's plan of salvation in Christ, Michal's despising David was more than the reaction of a haughty wife. David's words lead us to remember Christ, who took on human flesh and blood, who in humility became one of us to take our place under the Law and to obey it for us. To those who are proud in the world, the cross and the Savior who suffered in humbleness there are objects of shame. But to the poor in spirit, those who know our sin and our need for a Savior, the cross is held in honor.

Verse 23—Michal, who had reproached David, is now reproached by the Lord. His ultimate judgment was not merely that she would be barren—a status grieved by many women of all times—but rather that the Promised Seed, the King whose throne would endure forever, would not come through her.

3 A New House for the Lord (7:1–29)

Verses 1–3—As David got settled in his new fortress and palace, as he enjoyed a peace from enemies that he had not known for many years, he had time to think. It struck him as shameful that he lived "in a house of cedar, but the ark of God dwell[ed] in a tent." Upon hearing this, Nathan the prophet encouraged David to go ahead with his plans because the Lord was with him.

Verses 4–17—But God turned David's plan on its head. Nathan returned with a revised message, one that came directly from the Lord, not from Nathan's good wishes or "common sense." Instead of allowing David to build a house for the Lord, the Lord declared that He would establish a house—a dynasty—for David. In doing so, the Lord pronounced the most precious promise He ever made to David, a promise from which we all benefit. In these words, the Lord foretells the coming of His beloved Son, Jesus Christ, the King who will reign eternally. With these words, we reach the climax of David's life—and of ours. We will examine this messianic promise in detail in Session 9.

Verses 12–16—Through Nathan, God told David, "When your days are fulfilled and you lie down with your fathers, I will raise up your offspring after you, who shall come from your body, and I will establish his kingdom. He shall build a house for My name, and I will establish the throne of his kingdom forever. I will be to him a father, and he shall be to Me a son. When he commits iniquity, I will discipline him with the rod of men, with the stripes of the sons of men, but My steadfast love will not depart from him, as I took it from Saul, whom I put away from before you. And your house and your kingdom shall be made sure forever before Me. Your throne shall be established forever."

We may be aware that David's son, Solomon, completed the building of an earthly temple and continued David's dynasty. These words, however, find their most perfect fulfillment in Jesus Christ, descended from David. Jesus builds a house for God's name, to honor God's name, and He does so as He brings people to faith through His Word and in Holy Baptism (1 Peter 2:5–6).

Verses 18–29—David's prayer in response to God's promise manifests the kind of humbleness and faith that is the only proper way to praise and glorify God. God is truly glorified when we confess our need for Him and for His salvation.

It would be the height of presumption to think that we poor sinners could embellish upon God's work of saving us. We can only receive it by faith. But where the broken and contrite heart receives God's gifts, there God is truly honored.

That David received these blessings is obvious in the words of his prayer. He is so bold in this faith as to issue a command to God: (v. 25 NIV) "*Keep* forever the promise You have made concerning Your servant and his house. *Do* as You promised" (emphasis added). Where the Lord God has promised, we may hold Him to His Word, clinging to His grace forever.

4. A New Peace with Old Enemies (8:1–10:19)

The blessing about which David spoke finds a temporal expression as David subdues all his enemies. (8:6, 14) "And the Lord gave victory to David wherever he went." But as we will see, an even greater fulfillment would one day dawn on earth.

Conclusion

Have you already experienced the "golden years" of your life—or are they yet to come? In this unit, we have seen David in his prime. The Lord has given David peace and prosperity; he has victory over all his enemies and the respect of all the people. These successes, however, would be fleeting. David will end up being his own worst enemy. He will all too soon be on the run again, this time pursued by one of his own children.

Despite the fact that David's best years were short-lived, he could cling to something that was steadfast and eternal. God had promised to establish his house and his throne forever. That promise was fulfilled in Jesus Christ. We who are clothed in Christ through Holy Baptism have a share in that very same promise and kingdom. So if our golden years have passed or if they are yet to come—or even if we have no golden years at all here on earth—we can cling to the One whose throne is established forever. In Christ, the Lord ultimately gives us victory wherever we go, even as we go into death (Romans 8:37; 1 Corinthians 15:57).

Concluding Activities

Pray a prayer that flows from the words of Psalm 60:11–12—"Oh, grant us help against the foe, for vain is the salvation of man! With God we shall do valiantly; it is He who will tread down our foes."

Then distribute Study Leaflet 6 as you dismiss the group.

Lecture Leaders Session 6 | Life of David

David on the Edge

2 Samuel 11:1–12:31

Preparing for the Session

Central Focus

David had acquired many treasures, wives, and lands, but it was apparently not enough for his sinful nature. His lust gave way to adultery and murder. The prophet Nathan skillfully exposed David's guilt by applying God's Law. David repented, whereupon he found a gracious Lord who both forgave him and helped him face the consequences of his sin.

Objectives

That participants, led by the Holy Spirit working through God's Word, will

1. understand how David, in despising God's Word, despised the Lord Himself;

2. begin to appreciate the terrible consequences of sin; and

3. acknowledge their own sins and receive God's forgiveness through grace in Christ.

Note for the small-group leaders: Lesson notes and other materials you will need begin on page 74.

For the Lecture Leader

Session Plan

Worship

Begin the session with the hymn printed in the study leaflet. Accompaniments are available in denominational hymnals, such as *Lutheran Service Book* or *Lutheran Worship* (refer to hymnal index). (Note: Concordia Publishing House has available *Every Voice a Song*, a nine-CD set of organ accompaniments for 180 hymns and liturgy. All the initial worship hymns in the LifeLight courses are included in this resource. It's especially helpful for mission congregations and small parishes. See the list of study resources on p. 7.) Follow with this prayer:

Prayer

Almighty God, like David, we tremble before Your Law, which pronounces us guilty. And yet, like David, we also rejoice in the soothing balm of Your Gospel. When we stray, use Your ministers to restore us to You through repentance and faith. In Jesus' name. Amen.

Lecture Presentation

Introduction

Would you be willing to take a truth serum and then allow someone to ask you questions? How would you feel to be placed under oath and asked questions to which you must give complete and honest answers? Are there any "skeletons" in your closet that you would prefer not to have made public?

Most of us would not want our every sin to become public knowledge. We sometimes even try to cover them up, try to hide them. We may lie and deny if we are confronted or accused. And yet, even if we can avoid being exposed in front of other people, our sins can churn away inside of us.

David knew all about that. Listen to his words in Psalm 32:3–5:

> For when I kept silent, my bones wasted away through my groaning all day long. For day and night Your hand was heavy upon me; my strength was dried up as by the heat of summer. I acknowledged my sin to You, and I did not cover my iniquity; I said, "I will confess my transgressions to the LORD, and You forgave the iniquity of my sin."

In all the accounts about David we have read thus far, we have not seen any reason for a cover-up, for a denial of sin like the ones David describes in Psalm 32. Yes, he had married more than one wife, but God had not strictly forbidden that in Old Testament times. Yes, he had killed the inhabitants of numerous towns and villages, but Scripture never portrays David as a murderer.

But David's words in Psalm 32, and in other psalms too, lead us to conclude he had intimate familiarity with blatant and unconfessed sin. How did such a thing happen in the life of a "man after [God's] own heart"?

1 David the Adulterer (11:1–5)

The Lord God had been very clear in His prohibition of adultery (Exodus 20:14). In Matthew 5:27–28, the Lord Jesus explains the truth that adultery is a matter of the heart. He says, "But I say to you that everyone who looks at a woman with lustful intent has already committed adultery with her in his heart" (v. 28). David's adultery began from the very moment he set his eyes on Bathsheba bathing on the rooftop.

Verses 3-4—Every aspect of this account shows how flagrant David's sin was. First, without question, Bathsheba is married and not pregnant when David set his eyes on her. The man who answered David's inquiry about the identity of this beautiful woman told David explicitly that she was "the wife of Uriah the Hittite." Second, it was clear that she had been "purifying herself from her uncleanness." Leviticus 15:19–30 required a ceremonial washing after each month's menstruation, a ritual "uncleanness" according to the Old Testament holiness code. But even though he had heard the message, "David, she's married," loud and clear, David made choices—deliberate choices—that brought actual uncleanness, unholiness, and guilt into their lives. David led Bathsheba into sin. While one might argue that she could have refused, the fact remains that he inquired about her, summoned her, and slept with her. She did not approach him, nor—it seems clear from the text—would she have (v. 4).

Third, David's sin was not committed in the passion of the moment. In those days before the medical technology we enjoy now, Bathsheba could not have known immediately that she had become pregnant—it would have taken weeks. During that time, David lived with his sin, impenitent about it. By the time he learned of Bathsheba's pregnancy, he was well on his way to committing murder with as little concern for God's Law as he had shown when he committed adultery.

2 David the Murderer (11:6–27)

(Have the group look back to and read aloud 2 Samuel 10:7–9.) This particular battle may have held little significance for you if you had no previous or particular knowledge of the players involved in this drama. The fact that Joab selected some of the best troops in Israel and deployed them against the Ammonites and Syrians may not have grabbed your attention. But in fact what was happening in that battle was the murder of one particular man, Uriah the Hittite, the legitimate husband of Bathsheba. This murder, coupled with the adultery we just described, marked the lowest point of David's life.

In chapter 11, the same pitched battle is described in more detail from the viewpoint of David, who ordered it, and Uriah, who died in it. Their perspective is linked to the battle in 2 Samuel 11:1 and 12:26.

Verses 6-13—In the face of David and Bathsheba's unfaithfulness, Uriah shows himself to be faithful in every way. David imagines he can trick Uriah into thinking that the child conceived in Bathsheba's womb was his own, not David's. Innocent and honorable, Uriah did not cooperate, even when David got him drunk (v. 13)! Desperate to preserve his own appearance of righteousness (how like Saul before him!), David (vv. 14–15) resorted to underhanded violence. He schemed to salvage his own reputation by having Uriah killed by the hands of his enemies. Remember Saul's plan in 1 Samuel 18:17? Saul's plan against David failed, but David's plan against Uriah succeeded.

What unmitigated gall in David's encouraging words to Joab: (v. 25) "Do not let this matter trouble you, for the sword devours now one and now another." David further attempted to cover up his sins by feigning concern for Bathsheba, as if he, the "compassionate king," were taking a "war widow" into his house. In fact, he was taking his accomplice in adultery as his wife. The thing David had done "displeased the Lord" (v. 27). Would the Lord reject David as He had rejected Saul?

3 David the Penitent (12:1–12)

Many people today are deathly afraid of reporting a crime. They shudder at the thought of having to testify against criminals. They fear injury brought on by ruthless retaliation. As a result, they deny they have seen anything rather than face and accuse a guilty offender.

And yet, it doesn't take a hardened thug to make us reluctant to point out sin when we see it. Can you think of occasions when you have seen your neighbors or family members doing something unethical, but you failed to say anything because you were afraid they might get mad at you—or you might hurt their feelings?

If you recognize such fear in your own life, then you will appreciate all the more the task that the Lord gave

His prophet Nathan (v. 1). Nathan had to confront the powerful and popular King David, accusing him of his sin face-to-face. Had Nathan said nothing, David would certainly have continued in sin and could very well have died the eternal death of the impenitent.

Note that God's prophet did not rush to judgment. He could easily have gone into David's court, pointed his finger at David, and shouted accusations of adultery and murder. Nathan would have been right, but how do you think David would have reacted?

Verses 1–4—Nathan's sermon was one of the most profound and skillful uses of God's Law in all recorded history. Nathan aimed the Law at David's heart. It cut him to the quick, silenced him, and showed him his need—his desperate need—for a Savior.

Verses 5–6—David quickly pronounced an angry judgment on the unrighteousness he heard described in Nathan's parable: "The man who has done this deserves to die."

Verse 7—"You are the man!" Nathan replies in a moment of high drama. Some translations tack on an exclamation point, even though no such punctuation exists in the original Hebrew of the text. In fact, there is no reason to believe that Nathan raised his voice at all. He could have knocked David over with a feather even if he had whispered those words.

Nathan names from whom the indictment he delivers comes: (v. 7) "Thus says the Lord, the God of Israel." The indictment itself, straight from the judgment seat of heaven, was all too clear in David's eyes, now opened by Nathan's parable. By his own mouth, David had pronounced the verdict he deserved: death. The judgment of the Lord proclaimed by Nathan, however, might have seemed a fate worse than death. The rest of David's life would serve to illustrate in painful detail the destruction sin can bring into a life (vv. 10–12). The sword did not depart from David's house; his wives were given over to shame and abuse with those David thought were his allies. While David had sinned in secret, the consequences of his sin would show up (v. 12) in broad daylight.

4 David the Absolved (12:13–31)

David responded simply, (v. 13) "I have sinned against the Lord." Nathan made no comment. He did not elaborate or dwell on David's sin. He did nothing to suggest that David would be forgiven because he had shown how sorry he was—that would have been works-righteousness. He simply said, (v. 13) "The Lord also has put away your sin; you shall not die." Someone else, however, would die: the son he and Bathsheba had conceived in adultery. That may seem unfair to us. Why should an "innocent" newborn baby die because of sins that were not his own?

The answer to such questions lies hidden in the mystery of God's Son, Jesus Christ. Jesus had no sin, and yet God made Him (2 Corinthians 5:21) "to be sin." Was it fair for Jesus to suffer death that the world deserved? All talk about "rights" and "fairness" becomes superfluous in light of the Gospel. Salvation is not about fairness. It is about mercy.

Lest we too quickly apply the kind of consequences for sin David suffered to our own lives or to the lives of others today, remember that David was a public figure, the leader of God's people. His sin would surely become public knowledge, if it wasn't already so. The nations around Israel, who no doubt knew King Saul's obsession with destroying David, might well conclude that Israel's God let Israel's kings get away with murder. We can't know for sure that's why David's baby died, but it is one possibility (see v. 14).

As for the rest of Nathan's pronouncement in verse 11, note that none of this difficulty was to be God's doing. David's family problems, as well as his lack of leadership, attention, and love at home, would lead to the woes described here. The affair with Bathsheba was one more nail in the coffin of his relationship with his sons. Nathan announces the consequences—not "punishment" in the sense of revenge—David had set in motion by his actions.

Vv. 16–21—For seven days, David pleaded with the Lord about the baby. He refused to eat. He refused to get up from the ground. On the seventh day, the child died. At that news, David's servants feared that he would do something even more drastic. Instead, David got up, washed, worshiped the Lord, and sent for a meal. In doing this, David demonstrated the difference between sorrow and godly repentance. This difference bewildered his servants (v. 21), and it may well baffle people today. The apostle Paul makes this distinction in 2 Corinthians 7:8–10.

Verses 22–23—Worldly sorrow hates being caught and exposed. Worldly sorrow grieves the consequences of sin, sin's fallout, not the guilt of that sin and its offense before God. David did not dwell on his misery in the way that comes naturally to what Paul calls "worldly grief." Instead, David gets on with the life lived in faith, even to the point of confessing his hope for a reunion with his dead son in the life to come, (v. 23b) "I shall go to him, but he will not return to me."

Verses 24–25—David went to comfort his wife, Bathsheba, and he lay with her. She became pregnant by him again. But this son, legitimately conceived, did not die. He eventually succeeded David as king, completed the building of the temple, and expanded the boundaries of the kingdom of Israel to their furthest limits. David and Bathsheba named this son Solomon; the Lord, through the prophet Nathan, named him Jedidiah, "beloved of the Lord."

Verses 27–31—The city of Rabbah—which had given David the opportunity for adultery and murder—was now conquered by him.

Conclusion

As we close, a word about sin, consequences, and punishment is in order. Some people have taken David's story and used it as a bludgeon against those who suffer tragedy in their lives. Sometimes even Christian parents who have lost a child have used this account as a source of anguish. "What sin did we commit to have brought God's anger down upon our child?" they ask themselves.

Remember, God does not punish His children. He doesn't exact retribution from us for our sins. God punished Jesus in our place. Our sins are gone. He has removed them for us, as David says, (Psalm 103:12) "as far as the east is from the west." When evil strikes, it's natural to look at our hearts, to examine our conscience, for unconfessed sin. God does want us to bring our guilt to Him so He can remove it. But most times, when trouble strikes, it comes because we live in an imperfect world, a fallen world.

We serve a just God, a God who has already judged our sin—and removed it at Christ's cross. We need not live in fear over what punishment might lie just around the corner. Nor need we live in anguish over the problems in our lives as though they were God's verdict of condemnation.

Sin does, of course, sometimes have consequences in this life. Someone who robs a bank may go to jail. Someone who breaks the trust of a friend may find it hard—or sometimes even impossible—to win back that trust. But our gracious Lord helps His penitent children to bear those kinds of burdens. He goes with us—even to prison, if need be. He stays beside us always, assuring us that He is our faithful friend.

With David, we can pick up the pieces and go on with our lives. We can know for sure that nothing can separate God's repentant children from His love. No matter how awful our sin, no matter how horrible our guilt, no matter how heinous our crime—God forgives.

Concluding Activities

Pray a prayer that flows from the words of Psalm 51:10: "Create in me a clean heart, O God, and renew a right spirit within me."

Then distribute Study Leaflet 7 as you dismiss the group.

Lecture Leaders Session 7 — Life of David

David under the Sword

2 Samuel 13–22

Preparing for the Session

Central Focus

The consequences of David's sin produce havoc in his life. The members of his own household become his enemies. His kingdom lies on the verge of splitting apart. Those whom he had formerly conquered now rise again with menacing threats. In it all, David trusts the Lord to be his rock, fortress, and salvation.

Objectives

That participants, led by the Holy Spirit working through God's Word, will

1. witness the disintegration of relationships in David's household;

2. acknowledge the consequences of sin in their own personal relationships; and

3. rely on the Lord and His promises in the midst of personal trauma.

Note for the small-group leaders: Lesson notes and other materials you will need begin on page 77.

For the Lecture Leader

Session Plan

Worship

Begin the session with the hymn printed in the study leaflet. Accompaniments are available in denominational hymnals, such as *Lutheran Service Book* or *Lutheran Worship* (refer to hymnal index). (Note: Concordia Publishing House has available *Every Voice a Song*, a nine-CD set of organ accompaniments for 180 hymns and liturgy. All the initial worship hymns in the Life-Light courses are included in this resource. It's especially helpful for mission congregations and small parishes. See the list of study resources on p. 7.) Follow with this prayer:

Prayer

Dear Holy Spirit, You work through Your Word to restore us to faith in Christ and to a right relationship with our heavenly Father. Grant us Your grace and strength through the same Word as we bear the temporal consequences of our sin. We ask this through Christ, our Lord. Amen.

Lecture Presentation

Introduction

Most of us have probably seen a Gideon Bible in a motel or a hospital. In some of those Bibles, you may have found a sticker pasted on the inside cover by a radical group. This sticker raises the complaint that the Bible is a violent book. It attempts to make the case that the Bible ought to be kept away from children and other sensitive readers.

While we are likely to ridicule this position, after reading the portions of 2 Samuel covered in this unit, we might concede that there is some truth to what they claim. These chapters of 2 Samuel were probably not covered in much detail during your Sunday School years. The rape of Tamar and the revenge of Absalom are a bit too intense for tender-hearted readers. Why, then, did the Lord inspire the author to include such accounts in the pages of Holy Scripture?

Those of us who lead sheltered lives can be thankful that the Lord has spared us from violence. We ought not, however, have a naïve opinion about the world in which we live. We can find comfort in the fact that the Lord has proven His faithfulness in the midst of faithlessness on the part of sinful human beings. The contrast only magnifies His great mercy and grace. Furthermore, those who *have* suffered through dark days can take heart in knowing that, if the Lord can preserve David despite all his troubles, then He can likewise preserve us, His baptized children, through all of our trials.

1. Amnon's Repugnance (13:1–22)

David committed grievous sins—adultery and murder. He repented, and God, in grace, forgave him. But the consequences of his sin would be with him the rest of his life. Through Nathan, the Lord said, (12:10–11) "'Now therefore the sword shall never depart from your house, because you have despised Me and have taken the wife of Uriah the Hittite to be your wife.' Thus says the Lord, 'Behold, I will raise up evil against you out of your own house. And I will take your wives before your eyes and give them to your neighbor, and he shall lie with your wives in the sight of this sun.'"

Verses 1–5—That prophecy was to come true after a whole series of events were compounded by David's neglect of his responsibilities to his family. The first domino in the series of disasters began to tip when Amnon, David's oldest son and the heir apparent to his throne, began to look lustfully at his half-sister Tamar. It seems that perhaps precisely because Tamar was "forbidden fruit," Amnon wanted her all the more. Jonadab, Amnon's cousin, learned of this passion and wickedly advised Amnon to take her. One by one, the dominoes of that sin and its repercussions fell. Only the most torrid soap opera today could equal the events that took place under David's own nose.

Verses 6–14—Amnon feigned illness. In his ruse, he managed to trick David into letting Tamar come to his bedside. After Amnon sent all witnesses away, he grabbed her. Tamar pleaded with Amnon, suggesting that he marry her, hoping to deter him from rape. But his lust blinded him to all reason.

Verse 15–19—Then, as quickly as his so-called "love" had come, it was gone. In fact, he hated her more than he had loved her. Tamar grieved. Amnon had taken her dignity, her ability to trust, her virginity, and so much more. It was a heinous crime, one specifically forbidden by God's Law. Although David got angry (v. 21), he said nothing, did nothing. By his lack of action as both father and king, David compounded the wrong and, no doubt, the effects of Amnon's sin in Tamar's heart.

Amnon's actions enraged Absalom, Tamar's full-brother. Absalom offered advice to comfort her—advice he himself would not keep: (v. 20) "Do not take this to heart." So strong was Absalom's compassion and commitment to his sister that, years later (14:27), he would name one of his own daughters Tamar.

Absalom's anger quickly became hatred, coldly calculating hatred: (v. 22 NIV) "[He] never said a word to Amnon, either good or bad."

Absalom, you see, had decided to murder Amnon. In his mind, it was justifiable homicide. David's unwillingness to punish Amnon only fueled Absalom's fury.

2 Absalom's Revenge (13:23–14:33)

In both Deuteronomy 32:35 and Romans 12:19, God says, "Vengeance is Mine, I will repay." With those words, He forbids us to seek vengeance. But Absalom was not willing to leave the vengeance for his sister's suffering in the hands of the Lord. He waited two years for David to act. Then he took matters into his own hands.

13:23–39—Remember that Amnon had tricked David into letting Tamar come to his bedside. So now Absalom tricked David into sending Amnon to a sheepshearer's festival. Absalom did not bloody his own hands with Amnon's murder; he ordered his men to do it (v. 28). In the resulting melee (vv. 29–30), David's other sons fled. False rumors came back to David that all his sons had died. In verses 32 and 35, Jonadab set the record straight, but while David's other sons returned to David's courts (vv. 36–37), Absalom fled to the town of his grandfather Talmai of Geshur. Verse 39 tells us that David longed to go to Absalom after he was consoled concerning Amnon's death, but for whatever reason—pride, misplaced priorities, public opinion—King David left Absalom alone in Geshur.

14:1–24—Eventually, David's general, Joab, devised a clever ruse to get David to bring Absalom back to Jerusalem. Even so (v. 24), while Absalom lived in Jerusalem, David refused to see his son. (Think how awful it would be if our heavenly Father allowed us entrance to heaven, but forbade us to enter His presence!) Because of this, "home" wasn't home for Absalom. Heaven would not be heaven for us, either, without the presence of our heavenly Father. Thank God we *will* live in the light of His glory forever and ever!

Left on his own, Absalom found ways to get the attention he craved. On one occasion (vv. 30–32), he had Joab's fields set on fire to force Joab into a conversation with him. Absalom used this conversation to ask Joab to intercede with David on his behalf. As a result (v. 33), Absalom was finally restored to the courts of his father, the king. But David's outward show of acceptance and love was to be short-lived.

3 Absalom's Rebellion (15:1–18:18)

Absalom well may have considered his father weak for having failed to punish Amnon. Absalom's own return to public favor with David could easily have given the impression of weakness too. Absalom never stood trial for Amnon's murder. He didn't even apologize! There was no sign of repentance. But still, his public acceptance by David (14:33) meant that Absalom could again count on David's court to provide his livelihood. Thus, economically secure, Absalom set out (15:1-4) to undermine his father's popularity and ultimately David's throne itself.

Absalom's disloyalty and seditious talk went on (15:7) for four years! David may have heard of it, but he did nothing. So it can be no big surprise that, when we arrive at 15:13-14, we see David having to flee for his life because "the hearts of the men of Israel [had] gone after Absalom." As in his early years, David once again seeks refuge in the wilderness. Meanwhile, back in Jerusalem (16:22), Absalom knew all too well how to effect a change in the hearts of the Israelites, planting a vision of David's political impotence in every heart as he "went in to his father's concubines in the sight of all Israel."

15:30-31—Tearfully, David and his group of loyal followers proceeded up the Mount of Olives, barefooted, covered with dust—the very picture of grief and repentance. Centuries later, Jesus would sit on this same Mount of Olives as He sent His disciples to fetch some donkeys for His royal entry into Jerusalem. This mount was also the site of our Lord's betrayal. As Jesus, the King of kings, considered the abandonment and betrayal of His disciples on the Mount of Olives, He could easily have recalled David's experience centuries before. At the same place where Jesus would one day pray, (Matthew 26:42) "My Father, if this cannot pass unless I drink it, Your will be done," David prayed, (2 Samuel 15:31) "O LORD, please turn the counsel of Ahithophel into foolishness." When Ahithophel realized that Absalom had not followed his wise advice, he, like Judas centuries later, went out and hanged himself (2 Samuel 17:23).

Some of those who met David along the path of his flight proved to be faithful friends, like Hushai and Barzillai (15:32-37; 17:27-29), but not all. In 16:1-13, we read that some were opportunistic scoundrels, like Ziba, who took advantage of lame Mephibosheth, the son of Jonathan, whom David had vowed to care for. David was also plagued by a defaming fanatic named Shimei, who cursed David and pelted him with stones. In the latter instances, David allowed himself to be abused, cursed, and mocked in the same way that centuries later (Isaiah 53:5, 7) his descendant Jesus Christ would. Neither David nor Jesus would revile those who hurled insults.

18:1-15—When the time was right, David organized his men to fight the men of Israel in the forest of Ephraim.

(2 Samuel 18:5, 12-15) David had made it clear that Absalom was not to be harmed (vv. 5, 12), but when Joab came upon Absalom hanging helplessly in a tree, he acted in ruthless brutality (v. 14).

4 David's Restoration (18:19-22:51)

18:19-33—On two previous occasions (1:14-15; 4:9-12), David had responded harshly to those who thought they were bringing him good news of victory in battle and the death of his enemies. (2 Samuel 18:19-20) Joab did not think it a good idea to allow faithful Ahimaaz to take the news of Israel's victory and Absalom's death to David. So Joab sent a Cushite—a foreigner—instead. Ahimaaz overtook the Cushite (v. 22), running to tell the news of the battle to David, but the Cushite related the news of Absalom's death (vv. 31-32). On this occasion, David's reaction was not one of wrath, but of deep and bitter grief. He wailed over and over again, (v. 33; 19:4) "O my son Absalom, my son, my son Absalom!" Is there any grief deeper than that of a godly parent mourning the death of an ungodly, unrepentant yet beloved child?

19:1-8—David's grief totally demoralized his supporters. While they should have been celebrating a victory, they were plunged into deep shame and mourning. Joab's words were sharp, (19:6) "You love those who hate you and hate those who love you." David could easily have lost all his support that day, but (19:8) Joab's words sobered David. The king resumed his royal duties, even though his heart grieved over his son. God calls us too, at times to act in faithful service despite our feelings. We may be called on to give faithful witness to pure doctrine, even if it means feeling grief over people we love who refuse to respect and obey God's Word. We may, at times, need to set aside feelings of bitterness or anger so that we can act in love—perhaps Christlike "tough love"—toward those who need to hear the truth from our lips. We may at times need to use the strength God provides to speak words of confidence and faith, even when we don't at the moment feel like "God's person of great faith." The same Holy Spirit who enabled David to serve and lead God's people despite his feelings will also help us grieve, even while we serve others in Christ's name by doing those things He has asked us to do.

But 19:8-15, 40-43 tell us that just as David was restored to the throne, the feud between Judah and Israel flared up once again. In 19:16-39, David acted in mercy toward those who failed to help him in his time of need. He rewarded those who were found faithful. Chapter 20 tells us of one rebel who remained with a renegade band, but his head was soon thrown to Joab over the wall of the city in which he was hiding. In all this, David showed insight and diplomatic skill.

David's attempt to replace Joab with Amasa (19:13) would have been a diplomatic coup that could have gone a long way toward creating a united Israel. Amasa had served as Absalom's general, but David proposed making him the commander of his army instead of punishing him for treason! This was, no doubt, a great put-down to Joab, David's current commander. Joab had killed for much less than this, but his revenge on Amasa (20:8–13) was especially gruesome.

The chronological portion of 2 Samuel ends at 20:26. Chapters 21–24 form a kind of appendix. Several separate documents are recorded for us here. The first incident (21:1–14) occurred in the wake of a famine, which the Lord told Israel had resulted from Saul's blood-guilt. This account may have been placed in the record at this point to offset Shimei's curse and accusation (16:7b–8) that David was a "man of blood." David had shown that he was not a man of blood by sparing Shimei, and by the account in 21:1–14, which showed Saul as the true "man of blood," the one who did not honor the vow made to the Gibeonites.

The second account appended to this book (21:15–22) relates several battles between the Philistines and Israel. Because David had earlier subdued the Philistines (8:1, 11–12) and nothing more than historic reference is made of them in the chapters up to this point, it is probable that this account was added out of sequence, recalling David's earlier conquests. Of particular note in this section is the news that (21:19) "Elhanan the son of Jaare-oregim, the Bethlehemite, struck down Goliath the Gittite, the shaft of whose spear was like a weaver's beam." It is likely that Elhanan ("God is gracious") was another name for David.

Very similar in form and content, 2 Samuel 22 and Psalm 18 are a hymn of praise written by David when God had delivered him from all his enemies. David attributes all his success to the work of the Lord. The middle section (vv. 21–25), however, might seem troubling to those who consider it in light of all that we have read. David wrote things such as "The Lord dealt with me according to my righteousness; according to the cleanness of my hands He rewarded me." How could David have said such things in light of his adultery and murder? It was possible for David to speak in such a way only because the Lord's righteousness had supplanted David's own righteousness; the Lord's righteousness had, by God's grace, become David's own. David, who knew his sin very well, found great delight in the Lord's righteousness. Through the forgiveness of sins and the promise of God, the Messiah's holiness had actually become his own.

Conclusion

So it is, by God's grace, with us. Our Lord Jesus Christ has fully paid the penalty, taken the punishment for all our sin. He redeemed us "not with gold or silver, but with His holy, precious blood and with His innocent suffering and death." His forgiveness is full and free. We enjoy—right now—Christ's right standing before God as our very own.

When people imagine that the sicknesses and hardships that come upon them are some kind of punishment from God, they rob Christ of His glory. Christ suffered the full penalty for all our sins. God punished Jesus. Repentant sinners need never worry that He might punish us. Yes, we may endure earthly consequences that occur as a result of our sins. But even then, our Lord will walk beside us through them, even as He accompanied and strengthened David in his dark days. With David, we praise our Lord for His faithful love.

Concluding Activities

As you close, pray a prayer that flows from the words and imagery of Psalm 3:5–6: "I lay down and slept; I woke again, for the Lord sustained me. I will not be afraid of many thousands of people who have set themselves against me all around."

Then distribute Study Leaflet 8 as you dismiss the group.

Lecture Leaders Session 8 | **Life of David**

David at the Last

2 Samuel 23:1–1 Kings 2:46

Preparing for the Session

Central Focus

Before David "rests with his fathers" and is buried, he again invokes God's wrath and suffers at the hand of his son Adonijah. David succeeds, however, in establishing Solomon on the throne and advises him to observe what the Lord requires.

Objectives

That participants, led by the Holy Spirit working through God's Word, will

1. watch David struggle with temptation and sin until his life's end;

2. rely on the trustworthiness of God to forgive the penitent; and

3. encourage one another to gladly hear God's Word and rely on it for power to overcome temptation.

Note for the small-group leaders: Lesson notes and other materials you will need begin on page 81.

For the Lecture Leader

Session Plan

Worship

Begin the session with the hymn printed in the study leaflet. Accompaniments are available in denominational hymnals, such as *Lutheran Service Book* or *Lutheran Worship* (refer to hymnal index). (Note: Concordia Publishing House has available *Every Voice a Song*, a nine-CD set of organ accompaniments for 180 hymns and liturgy. All the initial worship hymns in the Life-Light courses are included in this resource. It's especially helpful for mission congregations and small parishes. See the list of study resources on p. 7.) Follow with this prayer:

Prayer

Merciful Lord, David was tempted in every way just as we are. And yet, You are merciful and forgiving both to him and to us, through Him who was likewise tempted, but who overcame sin, death, and the grave for us. Strengthen our faith and lift us up when we fall, for the sake of Jesus Christ, our Lord. Amen.

Lecture Presentation

Introduction

We began this study on the life of David seven sessions ago with the question "What events in your life do other people remember most?" Now, after our review of David's life, we have discovered much more than the fact that David killed Goliath and that he had an affair with Bathsheba. With so much more data—and in light of the significant events at the end of his life—we might now ask, "How would David have been remembered by his immediate family, surviving friends, enemies, and subjects?"

Just before General John Sedgwick was shot and killed on a Civil War battlefield, he reportedly said, "They couldn't hit the side of an elephant at this distance . . ." Perhaps you can think of other "famous last words," like these:

"Don't worry. I've done this plenty of times before."

"How could we possibly lose?"

"I don't see how it could do any harm."

"We don't need to turn off the circuit breaker—I can have this outlet rewired in a snap."

When your life draws to its close, what last words would you like to speak? What wisdom would you hope to impart to those who continue in this life after Jesus takes you into the next? As we meditate on the last days of David right now, think about what your own last words and acts will say to others about your Savior Jesus Christ.

1. David's Last Words (23:1–7)

The writer tells us that verses 1–7 were David's "last words." But we ask, "In what sense?" We find more words David spoke toward the end of his life in 1 Kings 1–2. In fact, the words of 2 Samuel 23:1–7 are not even the last recorded words of David in the Book of 2 Samuel! David had other things to say in chapter 24. But this song of David might well be considered last in the sense we might use the phrase "last will and testament." These are David's final words on the matter of his life. Perhaps they were also the last words that came from him in poetic form, in the form of a psalm.

The reformer Martin Luther wrote an entire treatise on the last words of David (*Luther's Works*, vol. 15, pp. 265–352). He comments, "How modestly David introduces his speech. He does not boast of his circumcision nor of his holiness nor of his kingdom, but he identifies himself simply as *the son of Jesse*. He is not ashamed of his lowly descent, that he was a shepherd. Yes, what is much more, he confesses his birth, in which he, like all men, came forth full of sin and guilty of death, for he wishes to speak of other matters, matters so sublime that no nobility of birth and holiness can be of advantage and no misery, whether sin nor death, can work harm" (p. 271). Luther went on to show in great detail how the work of the three persons of the Trinity is made exceptionally clear in these last words of David.

In these last words, David confessed once and for all what the Lord had done for him and for all of us, ruling in His righteousness. The words David spoke did not come from his own heart, but from the Holy Spirit, as David said, (v. 2) "The Spirit of the LORD speaks by me." The New Testament also attests to this fact. In Mark 12:36 (NIV), we read, "David himself, speaking by the Holy Spirit, declared." In Acts 1:16, Peter says, "Brothers, the Scripture had to be fulfilled, which the Holy Spirit spoke beforehand by the mouth of David." In Acts 4:25 (NIV), the believers pray, "You spoke by the Holy Spirit through the mouth of your servant, our father David."

In 2 Samuel 23:3, David writes, "When one rules justly over men, ruling in the fear of God"—but stop right there! Had David ruled justly, in righteousness? Not always. We've seen examples of grievous sin in David's life. But note that "justly" is not equated with what humans consider "good works." Rather it is paralleled with "the fear of God." Even here, David fell short. He did not always fully reverence and honor God. But a Perfect Ruler would come, One who would ultimately rule in righteousness. The Messiah would be born of David's line, and His reign would be eternal. His righteousness would be credited to David and to us—to all who by grace cling to God's promises.

Viewed out of context, David's words in 23:5 (NIV)—"Is not my house right with God?"—might seem to say that David was taking credit for having set his house in order, and thus that he deserved some credit from God. But we recall the very clear words of the Lord in 2 Samuel 7:11b–16. David's house was the work of the Lord. Remember what Nathan prophesied? (7:11b) "The LORD will make you a house." This house was the house of David's Greater Son, our Lord Jesus. The God David worshiped did fulfill His covenant with David in this Son (23:5b). That Son did bring salvation, and His "house" has increased tremendously—look at the Christian Church spread through all the world! We are a part of that Church, that eternal dynasty. This is the work of God, the fulfillment of His covenant with Abraham, Isaac, David, and all the Old Testament saints. But (vv. 6–7) all who reject the gracious reign of this King will be punished in eternal fire.

2. David's Last Sin (23:8–24:25)

23:8–39—Appended to David's last words is a list of his mighty men. These names and events may seem to be of little consequence to us—but that is perhaps all the more reason to take note of them. The Holy Spirit has seen fit to record these great deeds and mighty feats. We do well to keep our own lives in such perspective. Our names, too, are recorded in the Lamb's Book of Life. Those names and the things that we have by grace done in Christ's name will bring great glory and thanks to the Lord throughout all eternity. Not because we're so good—we're not; we're sinners—but because God is so good. He chooses to use us, to let us serve Him and then, wonder of wonders, in grace He rewards us for the "mighty deeds" He has given us and empowered us to do! He shares His glory with us! He gives us grace upon grace in our Savior, the Lord Jesus!

23:39—Note the name at the end of the list: Uriah the Hittite. His name would have seemed as irrelevant to us as that of Zalmon the Ahohite or Paarai the Arbite, except for the fact that Uriah's name reminds us of a singularly significant event. It reminds us of the depth of David's sin and the depth of the Lord's mercy—to David and to us.

The naming of David's mighty men serves as a bridge between David's psalm (23:1–7) and David's sin (ch. 24). It moves us from David counting on the Lord to David counting his army. God had given these men to David, but even so, note the emphasis on the fact that (23:10, 12) "the LORD brought about a great victory." In calling for the census (24:2) to be taken of all the fighting men, David had given himself over to thinking that Israel's safety and his own strength lay in the size of his army. When the dust settled (24:15), 70,000 men had died for this offense against the First Commandment.

The texts of 2 Samuel 24:1 and 1 Chronicles 21:1 begin the record of Israel's census by telling us that the Lord was angry with Israel—all of Israel, not just David. The whole nation seems to have fallen prey to the lie that their security lay with the size of their army. David ignored the advice of his general Joab: (2 Samuel 24:3; note the added detail found at 1 Chronicles 21:3–6) "May the LORD your God add to the people a hundred times as many as they are, while the eyes of my lord the king still see it, but why does my lord the king delight in this thing?" In 2 Samuel 24:4 and 1 Chronicles 21:4, we read that despite Joab's level-headed warning, David's royal—but sinful—will prevailed. David reflected the unbelief of his people. They trusted in themselves instead of in their faithful Lord.

Does our Lord find the same kind of unbelief in our hearts today? Do we as a congregation rely on the size of our endowment fund or on the bank accounts of a few wealthy members or on the personality of our pastor to keep the congregation going and growing? How about our personal lives? Do we trust the God who clothes the lilies of the field and feeds the sparrows to provide for us? Or do we rely on the stability of the company for which we work or the money we've invested or on the pension check we receive? Do we praise God for good health, or do we credit our insurance plan or our doctor or our good genes or our exercise program? Every good thing in our lives comes to us as a gift from God, the God who commands us to "fear, love, and trust in [Him] above all things."

Not all census-taking was sinful. In fact, the Lord God Himself had told Moses to number the Israelites (cf. 1 Chronicles 12:23–37; 23:1–27:34). What angered God was the attitude of David's heart and that of His people. In 2 Samuel 24:2, David had ordered that the census be taken from Dan (the far north of Israel) to Beersheba (the far south). In verse 15, the Lord countered with a plague that raged over the same territory. The Lord thus judged in such a way that Israel could not boast of numbers; the plague changed all the numbers!

David felt a great weight of guilt because of what his sin had brought upon the people: (24:17) "Behold, I have sinned, and I have done wickedly. But these sheep, what have they done? Please let Your hand be against me and against my father's house." In David's words, we hear echoes of our Lord's from His cross: (Luke 23:34) "Father, forgive them, for they know not what they do." David asked God to punish him in place of the people. Jesus Christ actually did die in the place of all people. Our Lord Jesus, great David's Greater Son, endured the anguish of death and of hell itself so that we need not bear it. David built that altar on the threshing floor of Araunah the Jebusite, the site upon which the temple would later be built. The plague stopped—at the place where the blood of animal sacrifices would serve as a reminder of the coming Lamb of God, the Lamb (Revelation 13:8 NIV) "slain from the creation of the world."

We read in 2 Samuel 24:24 and 1 Chronicles 21:25 that David insisted on paying Araunah the full price for the land he purchased, perhaps because the Lord had commanded His people not to take gifts from unbelievers to use as sacrifices or offerings (Leviticus 22:25; Genesis 14:22–23; 23:1–20). As we read 2 Samuel 24:24, we may have questions. Do we ever give God less than our best? Do we ever give from our leftovers, giving something that "costs us nothing"? Again, the outward appearance matters much less than the attitude of our hearts. Are our offerings motivated by the grace of God at work in our hearts? Or do we give to avoid feeling guilty, to look pious in the eyes of other believers, to impress our pastor? Only God knows. And only He can forgive our lack of sincerity, our lovelessness and cold hearts. Only He can change our attitudes and our actions so that they please Him, honor Him, and bring joy to us.

3 David's Last Wishes (1 Kings 1:1–2:12)

Nathan's prophecy (2 Samuel 12:10; 1 Kings 1:1–53; also compare 2 Samuel 12:11 with 1 Kings 2:21–22) that the sword would never depart from David's house did not end with Absalom's rebellion. In 1 Kings 1:6–8, we read that, like Absalom, David's son Adonijah was very handsome. In human terms, he stood next in the line of royal succession, being born after Absalom. He conspired with those who had been faithful to David: Joab and Abiathar. Zadok the priest, Benaiah the valiant fighter, and Nathan the prophet remained true to David (cf. 1 Chronicles 24:3; 2 Samuel 23:20).

2:1–9—After establishing Solomon as his successor, David charged Solomon with the duty to avenge him. The invectives David spews out against his enemies might well be understood in terms of prophecy. His words sound much like the words he prayed in his imprecatory psalms.

In 1 Chronicles 29:21–25 and 1 Kings 2:28–46, we learn that the nation acknowledged Solomon as king. Solomon did what David had, in justice, asked: Joab and Shimei were executed. Like Joab and Shimei, Abiathar (1 Kings 2:26–27) deserved to die, but instead Solomon removed him from the priesthood, thus fulfilling the prophecy the Lord had spoken to Eli the priest in the prophet Samuel's time (1 Samuel 2:27–36). God had sworn to remove the privileges of the priesthood from the ungodly family of Eli; Abithar was the last of Eli's descendants to fill that role.

Conclusion

2:10–11—The text says simply, "Then David slept with his fathers and was buried in the city of David. And the time that David reigned over Israel was forty years. He reigned seven years in Hebron and thirty-three in Jerusalem" (cf. 1 Chronicles 29:26–30). We have seen that many loose ends of Old Testament history were tied up at the end of David's life. Prophesies decades old were fulfilled. An era had ended; under King David the Canaanites were finally and fully expelled from the land the Lord had promised to Abraham centuries before.

As we close today, we, too, can tie up a loose end—the question with which we began this lecture. What do you want your final words, your last testimony, to be? What do you want to say to those who come after you, especially about the Lord Jesus and His faithfulness? Why wait until you find yourself on your deathbed? May God, by His grace, let your whole life—words and actions—even now sing of God's mercy and love in our Savior!

Concluding Activities

Pray a prayer that flows from the words of Psalm 138:7–8—"Though I walk in the midst of trouble, You preserve my life; You stretch out Your hand against the wrath of my enemies, and Your right hand delivers me. The Lord will fulfill His purpose for me; Your steadfast love, O Lord, endures forever. Do not forsake the work of Your hands."

Then distribute Study Leaflet 9. Make any necessary announcements and then dismiss the group.

David's Son, David's Lord

Selected Passages

Preparing for the Session

Central Focus

The promise of an eternal dynasty the Lord made to David is repeated time and again by Old Testament prophets and is ultimately fulfilled in Christ. Jesus Christ, David's Son yet David's Lord, will reign forever and ever. He provides a home for His people in His eternal kingdom, where we will no longer be disturbed or threatened.

Objectives

That participants, led by the Holy Spirit working through God's Word, will

1. understand that studying the life of David is not merely a historical or moral exercise, but essentially points us to Christ;

2. come to appreciate the numerous references to David made throughout Scripture; and

3. see themselves as beneficiaries of the Lord's promise to David.

Note for the small-group leaders: Lesson notes and other materials you will need begin on page 84.

For the Lecture Leader

Session Plan

Worship

Begin the session with the hymn printed in the study leaflet. Accompaniments are available in denominational hymnals, such as *Lutheran Service Book* or *Lutheran Worship* (refer to hymnal index). (Note: Concordia Publishing House has available *Every Voice a Song*, a nine-CD set of organ accompaniments for 180 hymns and liturgy. All the initial worship hymns in the Life-Light courses are included in this resource. It's especially helpful for mission congregations and small parishes. See the list of study resources on p. 7.) Follow with this prayer:

Prayer

Heavenly Father, we give You thanks and praise for Your servant David. By Your mercy, You chose him to point us to his Greater Son, our Savior Jesus Christ. Bless us now with the rich promises You have made for us as citizens of Your heavenly kingdom. We ask this through Christ, our Lord. Amen.

Lecture Presentation

Introduction

After having read the biography of a famous person, can you say that you really know that person? If someone were to write a book about you, would others know the "real you" after having read it? While the focus of this Bible study has been "the life of David," and while most of us have learned much more about David's life than we knew before, it would be an overstatement if we said that we really know David now. But "knowing David" was never the point.

The purpose of this study was not merely to know more about David. It was not to learn a bit of biblical history or even to learn moral lessons from David's life so that we could follow his example or avoid making his mistakes. And it was certainly not the intent of this study to lead people to pass some sort of judgment on David's life. (Romans 15:4–6) Rather, we recall that "whatever was written in former days was written for our instruction, that through endurance and through the encouragement of the Scriptures we might have hope. May the God of endurance and encouragement grant you to live in such harmony with one another, in accord with Christ Jesus, that together you may with one voice glorify the God and Father of our Lord Jesus Christ."

The point of studying David's life, of studying all the Scriptures, is to direct us to Christ—to the faith, hope, peace, and love that, together with David, we find in Christ alone. After studying the life of David for nine weeks, we must admit that we don't know everything about David—but we do know all the more about our need and about God's promise to meet that need in Christ.

Some people risk the dangers of shallow faith by living on the surface of the Bible instead of being nestled in the heart of God's living Word. Those who have not studied the life of David are missing out on some rich treasures for their own lives. Indeed, one can hardly read the Scriptures without bumping into David. According to one computerized search of the English Standard Version of the Bible, the proper noun *David* appears more frequently in the Bible than any other human name except Jesus (David 989, Moses 796, Abram/Abraham 287, Jesus 1058). This man David shows us what it is to need Christ. His life shows us what it means for a poor sinner to cling to the promise of Christ, to the faith and forgiveness that rest in the Messiah.

Thus, as we conclude our study and summarize David's life, we refrain from emphasizing the works of David. We must see in David's life the Word and work of Christ. The main highlights in this study, then, are not what David did for the Lord, but rather what the Lord did for David and what God has accomplished for us in Christ. The three key points we have seen are these:

1. The election and anointing of a shepherd king—1 Samuel 16:1–13.

2. The eternal promise of a house and throne established—2 Samuel 7:8–16.

3. The temporal consequences of sin—2 Samuel 12:10–12.

These elements run through the rest of the references to David in Scripture: in the Prophets, the Gospels and the words of the apostles.

1 David in the Prophets

2 Samuel 12:10—The sword continued to afflict David's house long after David's death. In 1 Kings 11:14, 23, 26, we see that, like his father before him, Solomon's reign was threatened by such adversaries as Hadad the Edomite; Rezon son of Eliada; and Jeroboam son of Nebat. After Solomon, the kingdom David had united was divided once again into the Northern and Southern kingdoms of Israel and Judah. The successors to David's throne were plagued by everything from murder to idolatry, and these conditions prevailed down through the centuries up to and including the time of Christ. In Luke 2:35, Simeon says to Mary, "a sword will pierce through your own soul." We might even defend the thought that this sword was itself evidence of the sword that came upon the house of David because of David's sin—and the sin of all human beings.

Throughout the remainder of the Old Testament era, the Lord sent His prophets to speak to the kings and people of Israel and Judah. Isaiah, Jeremiah, Hosea, Amos, and Zechariah occasionally called to mind the Lord's words of promise and warning to David, words that were made known to the people both during and after David's lifetime. What does one say to a people suffering under the weight of their own sins, people who were in some sense still experiencing the consequences of David's sins? Read 2 Samuel 24:11 and 2 Samuel 12:10. All the prophets spoke in the same way that Nathan and Gad had spoken to David—in words of Law and Gospel.

Over and over again the prophets referred to David.

Jeremiah 13:13; 17:25; 22:2, 4, 30; 29:16; 33:17, 26; 36:30—Jeremiah, for example, repeatedly refers to those who "sit on David's throne." This should have been a reminder of what the Lord had spoken to David in 2 Samuel 7:13 about establishing the throne of his kingdom forever.

Ezekiel 34:23–24; 37:24–25—Ezekiel was a prophet known to do and say radical things, but none more radical than to identify David with the Messiah:

"And I will set up over them one shepherd, My servant David, and He shall feed them: He shall feed them and be their shepherd. And I, the Lord, will be their God, and My servant David shall be prince among them. I am the Lord; I have spoken."

Romans 5:12–14; cf. Revelation 5:5—Thus, Jesus is not only the Second Adam, but He is also the ultimate David, the Shepherd-King for the salvation of all nations.

2 Samuel 12:11; Zechariah 12:7–8, 10, 12; 13:1—Again and again the prophet Zechariah refers to "the house of David," the house or dynasty that the Lord promised to establish. While the people of Judah were exiled in Babylon, Zechariah gave them a tender promise, one that talks about David and bears undertones of a crucified Messiah: (Zechariah 12:10)

"And I will pour out on the house of David and the inhabitants of Jerusalem a spirit of grace and pleas for mercy, so that, when they look on Me, on Him whom they have pierced, they shall mourn for Him, as one mourns for an only child, and weep bitterly over Him, as one weeps over a firstborn."

Isaiah 7:13–14—Isaiah, too, spoke of David's house when he foretold the coming Immanuel, "God with us." In other well-known messianic passages (Isaiah 9:7; 16:5), Isaiah speaks of David's throne being established—and that in the face of the oncoming Sennacherib, king of Assyria, who intended to subject David's throne to his own. To a people living under the shadow of impending doom and gloom, Isaiah prophesies: (Isaiah 55:3)

"Incline your ear, and come to Me; hear, that your soul may live; and I will make with you an everlasting covenant, My steadfast, sure love for David."

It would take a much longer lecture than this to unfold all the promises made about the Messiah, "David," and His people through the prophets. Suffice it to say that no one can rightly understand or fully appreciate the words of the prophets without knowing how the Lord dealt with David.

2 David in the Gospels

The Gospel of St. Matthew was originally written for those of Hebrew descent, people who knew their Old Testament Scriptures. The Holy Spirit had Matthew compose his Gospel in a way that would show that the intent of the entire Old Testament, with its threats and promises, was to direct the people of Israel to their Messiah, the Christ, the Anointed One.

From its opening verse and genealogy, David looms large. In Matthew 1:1, Jesus is introduced as "the son of David, the son of Abraham." In verse 20, the angel who appears to Joseph (Jesus' human step-father) calls him "Joseph, son of David." Unlike Luke, Matthew does not trace Jesus' genealogy all the way back to Adam but to Abraham through David.

Matthew does not list every single member of Jesus' lineage, but thematically arranges three groups of fourteen names each. (Matthew 1:17) "So all the generations from Abraham to David were fourteen generations, and from David to the deportation to Babylon fourteen generations, and from the deportation to Babylon to the Christ fourteen generations." Matthew places David as a central person in Christ's family tree. From chapter 1, verse 1, by the inspiration of the Lord, Matthew makes strong links between King David and Jesus Christ, who would ultimately fulfill the promises God made to David.

When one approaches Matthew's Gospel with a knowledge of the life of David, other things become apparent. In Matthew 2:2, for example, what comes to mind when you hear that the Magi come to worship "He who has been born king of the Jews"? This phrase takes on rich significance when viewed in light of the promise made to David in Samuel: (2 Samuel 7:13) "I will establish the throne of his kingdom forever."

Not only at the beginning of Matthew's Gospel is Jesus referred to as "the king of the Jews," but also toward the end we see the allusions. In Matthew 27:37, the account of Christ's crucifixion, we see the same phrase, "King of the Jews," used in reference to Christ. In His death and resurrection, Jesus Christ began to reign on the eternal throne God had promised David centuries before.

While the connection between David and Christ is especially prominent in the Gospel of St. Matthew, similar connections can be noted in the other Gospels as well. Keep the life of David in mind the next time you open the New Testament.

3 David and the Apostles' Teaching

The apostles, and Paul in particular, speak of David more in prophetic terms than in royal terms. Both Peter and Paul quote David's psalms as the inspired Word of God. David himself claimed: (2 Samuel 23:2) "The Spirit of the Lord speaks by me; His word is on my tongue." So the apostles noted as they prayed in Acts 4:25, "who through the mouth of our father David, Your servant, said by the Holy Spirit, 'Why did the Gentiles rage, and the peoples plot in vain?'"

Acts 2:29, 34; 13:34–36; Romans 1:3; 2 Timothy 2:8— The apostles also use both David's words and David's life to emphasize the doctrine of the resurrection. In Psalm 16:10, David wrote that God's Holy One would not see decay (corruption). Referring to this promise, Paul declared that David was not speaking about himself: (Acts 13:36–38)

"For David, after he had served the purpose of God in his own generation, fell asleep and was laid with his fathers and saw corruption, but He whom God raised up did not see corruption. Let it be known to you therefore, brothers, that through this man forgiveness of sins is proclaimed to you."

Many other allusions to the life of David can be drawn from the Epistles. See 2 Samuel 7:10–13; John 14:2–3; and 1 Peter 2:5. Think for instance about the words Nathan first spoke to David about the Lord establishing a "house" for him. Don't these words echo the themes of the apostles as they talk about an eternal house built of living stones?

An awareness of how the Lord unfolds His promises down through the centuries and ties them all together throughout the Scriptures deepens our awareness and appreciation of all that He has graciously done for us in Christ, to His great and eternal glory.

Conclusion

Many people today actively dig into the history of their family in order to find out about their family tree. No matter how far back you trace the roots of your earthly family, in Christ, we can go all the way back to David, to Abraham, and to Adam. Our family surname or the genetic markers in our blood have little to do with our *real* roots. John 8:38–48; Romans 9:7–8; and Galatians 3:7 tell us that, in Christ, we are children of Abraham. In Christ, we are royal heirs of the eternal kingdom God promised to David.

In this sense, the account of David's life is an account of our own lives. David's history is our history. The Jews at the time of Christ knew this, but we know it in an even deeper way by faith. For us, the life of David was more than David's life, because Jesus Christ, who is the life of David, is also our life.

Knowing all this, we rest secure. We are safe in life and death because of our Good Shepherd, our eternal King—the Messiah who died for us and rose again to give us life forever.

Concluding Activities

Pray a prayer that flows from Psalm 18:49–50: "For this I will praise You, O Lord, among the nations, and sing to Your name. Great salvation He brings to His king, and shows steadfast love to His anointed, to David and his offspring forever."

Then announce the next LifeLight class before you dismiss the group.

Life of David

Small-Group Leaders Material

Small-Group Leaders Session 1 | **Life of David**

A Messianic Mountaintop

1 Samuel 16:1–13; Psalm 23; Psalm 110

Preparing for the Session

Central Focus

God's plan of salvation proceeded through many generations from Adam to Christ. The life of David serves as one of the messianic mountaintops from which the whole range of God's work in Christ can be seen.

Objectives

That participants, led by the Holy Spirit working through God's Word, will

1. acquire a general overview of what is to come before embarking on a more detailed study of David's life;

2. appreciate the extraordinary circumstances of David's life—as well as the extraordinary means by which God sustained and protected David; and

3. examine their own lives in order to prepare them for the message of Law and Gospel proclaimed through God's dealings with David.

For the Small-Group Leader

Small-Group Discussion Helps

Day 1 • Various Passages

As you begin, note that this lesson is intended as an overview, an introduction to the life of David. In the weeks ahead, you will return to many details you will mention only this week. Encourage participants to keep track of questions that come to mind and to raise them during the appropriate class sessions to come.

1. The texts referenced in this question and in question 2 serve to summarize some of the main events in David's life. (a) Bethlehem. (b) Socoh in Judah, a.k.a., "the Valley of Elah." (c) David fled first to Samuel at Ramah. His flight then took him to various places—notably, the wildernesses of Engedi and Ziph, where David twice spared Saul's life. Later, David fled to Gath in Philistia, where the king gave him refuge in the town of Ziklag. (d) Hebron. (e) Hebron. (f) Jerusalem, also called the City of David or Zion. (g) David's palace in Jerusalem. (h) This question calls for an opinion. Ask volunteers to share.

2. (a) Absalom and Adonijah both tried to wrest the throne from their father—Absalom after killing another brother (Amnon) and returning from exile, and Adonijah when David was old, infirm, and vulnerable. These incidents hint at the terrible breakdown in David's family. (b) David passed along to Solomon the wisdom he had gained in a tumultuous lifetime; most especially the importance of walking in God's ways and keeping His commands. Though Solomon and his descendants were often unfaithful, God kept His covenant promises to David.

3. (a) As time permits, ask volunteers to read their summaries of David's life. Encourage the group to suggest events in which God was at work. (b) **Challenge question.** Answers will vary. The Lord promises to direct our paths. Help participants to distinguish, though, between a rigid, what-will-be-will-be view of life and the truth that God allows us freedom to make choices. Christians are not fatalists. We don't assume our lives are preplanned by our Lord to the nth detail. We do not live in fear that if we miss one detail we will scuttle His best for us forever. What a burden that would be! Instead, we know that our Lord promises to use each event in our lives to further His purpose for us—that we come to faith and become more like Jesus as His Spirit works in us through the Word. The word *purpose*, perhaps, explains these truths better than the word *plan*.

Day 2 • Various Passages

4. (a) Matthew names some of David's notable ancestors: Abraham, Isaac, Jacob, Judah . . . Boaz (Ruth), Obed, Jesse. Let participants comment on the blessings and burdens that might come with such a rich heritage, as well as offer observations about their own family heritage. (b) The first nine chapters of 1 Chronicles are genealogies. The Chronicler lists David's brothers as Eliab, Abinadab, Shimea (a.k.a., Shammah or Shimei), Nethanel, Raddai, and Ozem. David was the youngest of Jesse's sons. Again, let volunteers comment on the pros and cons of growing up as the youngest of seven

sons in a large, extended family. The 1 Samuel 17:12–30 text hints at the rivalry or condescension David experienced. (You may want to mention that David's family tree is printed out in the enrichment magazine.)

5. In all probability, the families of group members are not as extended or complex as David's, yet blended families and their complexities are a reality today. Encourage participants to share ways they can and do influence family members, their church, and the wider community for good. Perhaps they set an example by their worship and prayer life. Maybe they nurture children; provide wise counsel; or encourage, guide, and support other family members. Maybe they are proactive in seeking outside help when necessary. As time allows, discuss ways to influence family via "long distance."

Day 3 • Various Passages

6. (a) Answers will vary. (b) Encourage comments. Ask participants to explain their reasons for the choices they made. Compare responses. Think about how Samuel's anointing must have influenced David, how his fame as a giant-killer would have affected him, the survival skills he must have learned "on the run," and the power he exercised as warrior and king. Include also the guilt and grief he experienced later in life because of his sin.

7. *For personal reflection. Sharing optional.* Encourage sharing, but avoid making anyone uncomfortable. Perhaps some have drawn a timeline in their study leaflet and would be willing to share it with the group. Point out that sometimes events that seem bad (or even disastrous) to us as we walk through them turn out to influence us for good, to drive us to the Scriptures and to the Sacrament, where God strengthens our faith, or to make us more sensitive to the distress and needs of others. Share an example from your own life, if possible.

Day 4 • Psalm 23

8. (a) When David was on the run from Saul, hiding in caves, among the rocks, or in the wilderness, he surely must have longed for the green pastures and still waters of his boyhood shepherding days. Accept other reasonable answers. (b) Saul was David's enemy, but others sought his life too—the Amalekites (1 Samuel 30), the Philistines (2 Samuel 5:17–25), traitors like Sheba (2 Samuel 20:1–22), and even members of his own household (2 Samuel 15:10–12; 1 Kings 1:5–6). David's life was often in danger. Yet, never was he more in jeopardy than when he rebelled against God and committed murder and adultery. In peril of eternal death, he admitted his guilt (2 Samuel 12:13–13) and God forgave him, restoring his soul. Accept other reasonable responses.

9. David truly did want for nothing. The Lord provided for all of David's needs: rest, nourishment, refreshment, encouragement, guidance, security, prosperity, and—best of all—His righteousness. As you and your group study David's life in detail during the weeks to come, all this will become more clear.

10. *For personal reflection. Sharing optional.* Encourage your group to pray for one another each week. If participants are receptive, make a list of prayer requests at this point. God gave us His Son, Jesus Christ, and through His life, death, and resurrection, Christ won the victory over sin for us. Through the gift of His Holy Spirit working in His Word, He creates and sustains faith in our hearts. The same Spirit guides us daily as we live in the grace of our Baptism. His Holy Supper strengthens us for holy living. In addition to all these precious gifts, God gives us to one another. As Christians, we love and care for one another in body, soul, and spirit.

11. (a) God invited David to His banquet, even while David's enemies raged against him. (b) David had many enemies—Saul and his supporters, warring neighbor nations, and even members of his own family. Yet, in the midst of danger, God renewed His promise to protect and prosper David. Moreover, He promised an everlasting kingdom to the house of David; this was fulfilled in the kingship of Christ, who was born of the tribe of Judah, the house of David (2 Samuel 7:8–16). (c) God is hospitable indeed! Note that we share in the fruits of God's promise to David. Christ is our Savior too—an overflowing cup of blessing even as we face sin, Satan, and death—our worst enemies.

12. Our Lord Jesus, the strong victor over sin and death, hosts us poor sinners at His Table. In the bread and wine of Holy Communion, He gives us His own body and blood, the forgiveness of sins He earned for us on the cross, and strength to live out our new relationship with Him. We are weak, but He is strong; and He shares His strength with us so we can defeat the enemies of darkness we face each day.

13. Encourage participation. We have eternal life now, and we can confidently anticipate life in heaven after life on earth is over—not because "we tried our best" or "came to church" or did anything else in an effort to earn eternal life. We can be confident only because, by grace through faith in Jesus Christ and His atonement, we are children of God and heirs with Christ.

Day 5 • Psalm 110

14. Participants may suggest that David acknowledged the coming King (Christ) would be his (David's) superior. The coming King would be victor over His enemies. His kingdom would stretch far and wide. His "warriors" would be willing to sacrifice for Him. His would be the highest of priesthoods. He would judge those He vanquished and rule in the highest position forever. Accept other answers drawn from the text.

15. In Mark 12:35–37, Jesus quotes Psalm 110, showing that the Messiah was more than a descendant of David; He was also David's Lord. Most people of that day knew the Messiah was to be a descendant of David (Isaiah 11:1–3; Jeremiah 23:5–6; Ezekiel 34:23–24). Here, Jesus identifies Himself as the fulfillment of that prophecy.

16. Peter quoted this psalm of David in his sermon on Pentecost. Peter showed that David understood how powerful, worthy, great, and divine his descendant would be. Peter connects David's prophecy with "this Jesus" whom the Jews crucified and who is now resurrected and exalted. Peter's appeal, by the power of the Spirit, moved people to repentance and faith.

# David on the Field

1 Samuel 16–18

Preparing for the Session

Central Focus

The Lord delivers His people in unusual and remarkable ways. In times past and still today, God chooses and uses unlikely people—sinners, all—to accomplish His purposes.

Objectives

That participants, led by the Holy Spirit working through God's Word, will

1. see that God works in surprising ways;

2. develop a stronger confidence in God when threatened;

3. do everything—in word and deed—in the name of the Lord; and

4. trust God's work on their behalf in Christ.

For the Small-Group Leader

Small-Group Discussion Helps

Day 1 • 1 Samuel 16:1–13

1. (a) Saul's heart was filled with rebellion, and he was focused on himself, on self-promotion. Rather than listening to the Word of the Lord spoken by the prophet Samuel, Saul decided which part of which commands to obey and which to ignore. This rebellion was "as the sin of witchcraft" (1 Samuel 15:23 KJV) because it broke the First Commandment—Saul made himself god. (b) As judge and prophet, Samuel was God's spokesperson and God's "arm," His representative in Israel. Samuel was, by grace, God's obedient servant. Samuel had attempted to guide and correct Saul, and like a father, he grieved over Saul's failure to live up to God's calling in his life. Samuel recognized Saul's jealous ego and his potential for violence. Yet, Samuel obeyed God and went looking for "him whom [God would] declare to you" (v. 3), thus allowing himself to be led by God despite the very real danger this could bring. Accept other observations drawn from the text.

2. (a) Bethlehem's elders may have trembled in fear, thinking Samuel as God's spokesperson had come to point out some corporate sin. Perhaps they worried that as God's prophet, Samuel would pronounce judgment on them. Accept other reasonable answers. The point of the text seems to be that Samuel was highly respected and perhaps even feared in Israel. (b) **Challenge question.** The two texts cited, along with multiple others in the New Testament, describe a mutual relationship of love, respect, and care. The pastor in a Christian congregation will one day "give an account" to God (Hebrews 13:17) for his ministry. Because the pastor has God-given responsibility for immortal souls, the Lord also has given pastors authority to speak and act for Him. We "obey" and "submit" in spiritual matters in line with the Word of God. But pastors also can fall into temptation. Peter warns pastors not to be "domineering over" the flock (v. 3), not to try to force or demand obedience and respect from unruly, unwilling "sheep." Instead, Christ's undershepherds are to serve, willingly and eagerly (v. 2), and to go the extra mile in love for those for whom Christ died. They are to avoid greed. Pastors and people alike are to set a good example of humility, love, faith, and self-control. Peter's exhortations to people and pastors are tied together in verses 8–9—his reminder that we have a common enemy, Satan. As we watch and pray for one another, we can thwart Satan's schemes to destroy both Christ's flock and its human shepherds.

3. (a) The people of Israel soon recognized in David a gifted musician and warrior (v. 18). These gifts of the Spirit would empower him to deliver and later rule God's people. (b) Answers will vary. Encourage participants to share their thanks with those whom God uses to touch their lives.

4. (a) David, the youngest in his family, appears humble, obedient, and responsible. Christ's presence in our heart makes it possible for us to reflect love, selflessness, generosity, honesty, and faithful behavior. Without these characteristics, we reflect our Savior poorly. Our service and witness have no power. (b) Ask only volunteers to share their thoughts or share your own. Don't put anyone on the spot. But do share the Gospel with

Small-Group Leaders Session 2 — Life of David

one another. In Christ, God can and does forgive our proud unteachableness. In Christ, He can and does empower the humility and genuine openness to direction and correction we identify as teachableness.

Day 2 • 1 Samuel 16:14–23

5. (a) Satan rules the kingdom of darkness. (b) Paul directed that the impenitent person be excommunicated from the congregation in Corinth and thus placed outside the protection of Christ and vulnerable to Satan's attacks on his body, mind, and soul. (c) While this sounds harsh, unloving even, Paul (and the Lord) had only the sinner's ultimate good at heart. The purpose was that the sinner repent of his incest and ask for God's pardon. In Christ, he would be forgiven and restored. Excommunication can be seen as "severe mercy"—severe in the sense that it has dire consequences, serious ones indeed, but mercy in the sense that it represents an all-out, last-ditch effort to rescue the sinner by awakening him or her to the dangers of impenitent sin. (d) The same dynamics seem to be at work in the Spirit of the Lord leaving Saul. God was doing everything He could do to shake Saul awake and bring him to repentance. By his rebellion, Saul rejected the Holy Spirit. Soon an evil spirit took up residence in his heart. Realizing he had lost favor with God, Saul likely suffered from regret, guilt, depression, and fear. He lashed out in suspicion and fury, blaming others, especially David, for his own weakness and failures. Bitter, troubled, and perhaps tormented by nightmares or hallucinations, Saul became a pitiful man.

6. (a) Surprisingly, the young man who poses the most serious threat to Saul's throne is the person God uses to quiet Saul's misery. The Spirit of the Lord, alive in David's music, soothes Saul's suffering. Saul himself invites David, a simple shepherd, to his royal court. (b) Encourage those who are willing to tell about times when God's actions in their lives surprised them. In the life of a Christian, nothing happens merely by coincidence. God often directs and uses the events of life for our good and His glory. Share an example from your own life as time permits. (c) Allow participants to share. In Christ's cross, we see that God loves us unconditionally. His mercy and goodness meet us at every one of life's twists and turns. As we recognize God's forgiving love in Christ acted out for us over and over, day after day, our confidence and trust in His love grows deeper. We realize that His Word is true—for us personally, as well as for humanity in general.

7. David was a gifted musician. He was also a brave warrior, well-spoken, and fine looking. The Lord was with David. Encourage everyone to suggest the quality they feel most significant for David's future and to explain why. Stress the Lord's work in David's personal history. God's grace and power made it possible for David to accomplish God's purposes. Beauty fades, youthful strength will disappear, but God's grace and the strength of His purpose never changes.

Day 3 • 1 Samuel 17:1–51

8. (a) Although a favorite at court, David continued to tend his aged father's sheep. He obediently carried provisions to his brothers in Saul's army. He showed maturity and responsibility in the way he obeyed his father and as he handled his father's affairs. (b) David proposed to fight Goliath himself. David was confident in God's power to deliver His people. He told Saul that God had already empowered him to kill a lion and a bear. Goliath dared to defy God (v. 26), but David saw the situation with clarity: "The battle is the Lord's" (v. 47).

9. (a) David's youth, size, and lack of experience made him an unlikely match for the seasoned warrior Goliath. (b) David's weapons were, on a human level, no match for those of Goliath.

10. (a) Circumcision served as the seal of God's covenant promises to His people. David stood up to the giant because he saw Goliath as an enemy of the living God (v. 26). (b) Goliath had no such covenant with the living God. Instead, Goliath blasphemed God's honor. Goliath scorned God's covenant promises to Israel (v. 26). (c) David knew he could rely on the Lord's protection and that Goliath had no such help. (d) David defied Goliath out of respect for the Lord, out of concern for the Lord's reputation among his own people and among the Philistines.

11. God is the only hero in all Scripture. Humanly speaking, David was doomed. But the Lord's power enabled David to kill Goliath and deliver God's people. Point out that we poor sinners can never deliver, save, or protect ourselves. Our hero is God, who acted in Jesus Christ to save us from our sins and who still acts to help us in every time of need.

12. *For personal reflection. Sharing optional.* Some members of your group may want to share what they have written. Others may not. Respect each person's privacy. Possible responses for (a) include illness, addictions,

debt, unemployment, abuse, phobias, broken relationships. (b) Assure one another that through Christ, God has won the battle for us. Satan, sin, and death have been defeated. Romans 8:31–39 assures us that God is for us. He is on our side. He wants only the very best for us. He proved His love by giving His only Son to die in our place. Now nothing we fear can ever separate us from His love. As David grew older, he understood more and more fully the threats listed in Romans 8:35. Yet, he wrote of God in Psalm 31:5, "Into Your hand I commit my spirit," and Psalm 31:15, "My times are in Your hand." Jesus echoed David's words as He died for us on the cross (Luke 23:46). Because of Jesus' redeeming love, we can in trust, also commit our spirits—indeed, our entire lives—into our heavenly Father's hands. You may want to ask a volunteer to read Romans 8:31–39 aloud before you go on.

Day 4 • 1 Samuel 17:51b–18:5

13. (a) David defied Goliath, facing him in battle with only a slingshot and the Word of God. David also gave a powerful verbal witness to all who would listen, while he continued to discount Goliath's ability, pointing out that Goliath was "uncircumcised"—Goliath had no covenant with the Lord. (b) We need to remind ourselves often of who we are and whose we are in our Baptism. That covenant with our Lord cuts otherwise unbeatable enemies (sin, Satan, and death) down to size. In Jesus and His cross, we have become overcomers. Baptism links us to Christ's cross and open tomb (Romans 6:1–14). Let the group share practical tips for recalling Baptism's power (e.g., making the sign of the cross, framing and displaying one's baptismal certificate, memorizing pertinent Bible verses and using them in times of temptation).

14. By God's design, David was introduced to Saul's court; his relationship with Saul developed through David's skill in music. David witnessed to Saul, to Goliath, and to both the Israelite and Philistine armies regarding God's faithfulness. By God's power, David won a tremendous military victory, and he won over the hearts of his people by delivering them. This victory must have encouraged David and helped him understand the meaning of his anointing. He gained widespread "name recognition." In all these ways, he was primed for a position of national prominence.

15. (a) David took on Goliath "in the name of the Lord" (17:45). David acknowledged God's power and trusted in Him. David did what he did for God and for the good of God's people. Even in the smaller details of life (respect for his father; the way he did his daily mundane duties), he acted "in the name of the Lord." As you discuss this question, repeat again the truth that God's grace made all this possible. David is not the hero of these accounts; God is. (b) Encourage everyone to share responses. Our Savior Jesus lived a life of purpose designed by His Father. Jesus served God and His people. We want to do the same. Everything we say and do can reflect our thanks to God for the gift of His Son. Call attention to Colossians 3:16. Note that being grounded in the Word comes first. Talk about how LifeLight Bible study helps your group grow in faith and life. (c) *For personal reflection. Sharing optional.* Encourage general comments rather than specific, personal examples. When we realize we are "in Christ," we begin to understand that nothing, not even death, can ultimately harm us. Safe in the cross of Jesus, we can approach all of life's challenges with the kind of confidence and commitment God gave David.

Day 5 • 1 Samuel 18:6–30

16. David's successes pleased Saul's army (v. 5), the townspeople (vv. 6–7), and the entire nation (v. 16). His name was well-known, even to Israel's enemies (v. 30).

17. Saul was evidently seething with jealousy (vv. 8–9), so much so that he tried to murder David (vv. 10–11). He deliberately put David in jeopardy (vv. 17, 21, 25). Saul was also afraid of David and of David's success. Saul knew God had left him and now was with David (v. 12). Saul saw even the loyalty of his own family slipping away (vv. 28–29). Still, Saul's core problem was not David's growing prominence, but his own unrepentant heart and his estrangement from God.

18. **Challenge question.** Jesus taught that all sin, jealousy too, comes from our hearts. The heart is where we must begin if we are to purge jealousy from our lives. First, led by God's Spirit to see our sin, we confess it to God without excuse. Then, remembering Christ's cross, we trust His forgiveness and ask Him for power to overcome this sin. We may need to repeat this process daily, hourly, or every five minutes. But God promises to keep on forgiving and strengthening us. He will give us the victory—in fact, in Christ, we have already won! Only in this Gospel truth will we receive the power we need to break sin's grip on our lives. We are powerless in and of ourselves.

19. (a) Saul may have wanted to keep an eye on David, ride the coattails of David's high approval ratings, and possibly have occasion to assassinate David. (b) David responds to Saul's offer with humility. Possibly he sensed Saul's ulterior motives. Or it could be he was unable to pay the bride-price. (This was a fee paid to the bride's father as compensation and insurance against her widowhood.) Maybe David was being shrewd in dealing with Saul. Let participants offer opinions. We can't really tell from the text. Stress the ways in which Saul and David reveal their human frailties.

20. This question summarizes the week's study. The child of God can live confidently and righteously before God because Christ lived a life of righteousness for us. He paid the penalty for our sin and reconciled us to our heavenly Father. He won the victory over Satan, sin, and death for us. Now nothing can rip us from His Father's arms. By faith, these gifts are ours. Fear need torment us no more! Our Baptism assures us we belong to God, that our sins are forgiven, and that the Spirit of the Lord lives within us—in power. Through daily repentance and forgiveness, we greet each new day confident that the Holy Spirit will empower us for a life of faith, obedience, and service.

David on the Run

1 Samuel 19–31

Preparing for the Session

Central Focus

When we suffer unjust attacks, we can endure in patience, waiting for God to act on our behalf. We can rely on His gracious promise never to fail or forsake us.

Objectives

That participants, led by the Holy Spirit working through God's Word, will

1. follow David's movements as he flees from Saul;

2. trust God's care on the basis of the promises in His Word;

3. develop restraint when dealing with adversity; and

4. learn to patiently respect authority, even when those exercising it act in difficult or distressing ways.

For the Small-Group Leader

Small-Group Discussion Helps

Day 1 • 1 Samuel 19–20

1. Jonathan served as a go-between, a buffer between his father and his friend. Saul tried to make Jonathan his accomplice, but Jonathan remained loyal to David and spoke up for him (19:4–5). Jonathan seems to have been unselfish and free of personal ambition. He seems to have understood and accepted David's destiny. He acted as an informant for David and cooperated in a scheme to deceive Saul. He put himself at risk for David's sake. At first, Jonathan's influence seems to have been effective (v. 6). But soon, Saul made the first of many broken promises not to harm David.

2. Jonathan's friendship and Michal's love were both signs of God's favor toward David. On a purely human level, even Saul's children recognized the irrationality of his insane jealousy. Clearly God used them both to save David.

3. (a) The Spirit of God incapacitated Saul so that he could not harm David. In the Old Testament, the word *prophesying* is sometimes used to indicate uncontrolled, ecstatic behavior. (See 1 Kings 18:29 for an example of heathen prophets engaged in this behavior.) It can also mean an enthusiastic praising of God inspired and animated by the Holy Spirit. Each previous delegation Saul had sent after David also was deterred by such prophesying. Clearly God was at work. (b) In 1 Samuel 19:23–24 and 10:1–13, we read about the Holy Spirit filling Saul and Saul apparently prophesying. In 10:1–13, the Spirit came on Saul to equip him for service to God's people. But Saul's attitude changed from one of reverence and obedience to one of fear and paranoia (19:24). How far he had fallen! Saul abandoned any hope in God. This unbelief grieved God, but God continued to work in Saul's life in an effort to bring him to repentance anyway; this seems to be what 19:24 is all about! Saul's refusal to repent makes the story of his life a great tragedy.

4. Let volunteers comment. The names for God will vary with the translations participants use. Accept comments that grow from the text.

5. From 1 Samuel 18:10 to 20:42, Scripture records seven attempts by Saul to murder David. As the study leaflet states, the number seven often symbolizes completion or totality in Scripture. (a) In 18:10–16, Saul threw a spear at David; in 18:17–30, Saul tricked David into fighting with the Philistines, hoping they would kill him; in 19:1, Saul commanded his son and servants to murder David; in 19:8–10, Saul again threw a spear at David in an attempt to pin him to the wall; in 19:11–17, Saul sent a group of servants to assassinate David while he slept; in 19:18–24, we read that Saul sent three groups of assassins, then went himself; finally, in 20:1–33, Saul tries to convince Jonathan that it's in Jonathan's personal interests to kill David, but when Jonathan remains loyal, Saul attempts to kill Jonathan! (b) The holy writer includes seven examples, possibly to communicate the idea that Saul's hatred was total and his commitment to kill David was unadulterated by mercy or repentance.

Day 2 • 1 Samuel 21–23

6. (a) David and his men survived by eating the consecrated bread from Ahimelech the priest at Nob. (Notice that Jesus tacitly approved this otherwise unlawful survival tactic, in Matthew 12:3–4.) Twelve fresh loaves of bread were placed in the tabernacle (later the temple) each day. They were an offering consecrated to God as a symbol of God's provision for Israel, His people. This appears to have been an act of faith in God's promise that he (David) was the Lord's anointed. Jesus' approval seems to bear this out. (b) David survived by escaping to Gath and pretending to be insane. The king's servants recognized David and may have tried to detain him against his will if it hadn't been for his ploy. This seems to be an act of folly based on fear. David's alliances with the Philistines later led David to the brink of treason (28:1–2). (c) David survived by hiding in the cave of Adullam. He set up a paramilitary force of sorts, organizing a group of debtors and malcontents. At this point, about four hundred men had joined him. David in faith obeyed God's prophet Gad (v. 5) and hid in the forest of Hereth.

7. (a) Answers will vary based on which psalm each participant chooses. As time allows, let volunteers share their answers. (b) Again, let volunteers share. Help participants compare their own lives with David's. Emphasize the fact that we, too, can seek God's will, trusting Him with our fears and frustrations. We, too, want to be firmly rooted in God's Word so that even when times of trouble come, we can in peace rely on God's unfailing love.

8. (a) Saul's relentless pursuit and confirmed reports of his murderous intent must have sapped David's physical and emotional strength. After all, he was just a human being—like any one of us! How encouraging to David that his friend should appear in person to shore up his courage and resolve—not in might or military strategy, but "in God." Jonathan brought David reassurance in God's promise: "You shall be king" (v. 17). (b) Focus discussion on what the encourager said or did. What was helpful? What was not? Why? Words such as "Everything will be all right" usually don't do much good. But sharing God's Word, God's promises of grace and help, in a simple way can bolster fainting hearts like nothing else. (c) Let volunteers share their thoughts.

9. Draw out examples. As we dig deep into God's Word, He communicates with us, His children. Believers today have an even fuller revelation of God's good and gracious will in our Savior Jesus Christ. Also, we have the blessings of the Sacraments. God uses His Word and Sacraments to assure us that He has made us His friends in Christ. We want to avail ourselves of these His gifts and live in friendship with our God every day of our lives.

Day 3 • 1 Samuel 24–25

10. (a) Because David respected the Lord, he refused to raise his hand against the king God had chosen. David prevented his men from attacking Saul. Even when they had what looked like the perfect chance, David was conscience-stricken for his audacity in trimming Saul's robe! (b) David explained to Saul that he had resisted the advice of his own men because Saul was "the Lord's anointed." He called Saul "lord" (v. 8) and "father" (v. 11)—terms of respect. In all this, he proved his own innocence. Instead of relying on human schemes and reasoning, he called on God to vindicate him. In all this, David clearly restrained his own tendency toward revenge and bitterness. Instead, David waited for the Lord to act. Guide participants to compare David's response to theirs in similar situations. Talk about the importance of

• respectfully confronting someone who is abusing you;

• sifting the advice others give, comparing it with the Word of God;

• reflecting on the God-given authority in the situation;

• continuing to communicate calmly and respectfully;

• explaining your own feelings and behavior clearly; and

• trusting God to act.

12. Nabal's insult seems a misdemeanor in comparison to Saul's offense. David restrains himself with Saul ("the Lord's anointed"), yet blows up at Nabal. His ongoing respect toward Saul seems all the more significant when compared with his reaction to Nabal. David was evidently not one to take insults and disrespect lightly.

13. Abigail encouraged David (v. 29). She reminded him of God's promise (v. 30). She showed him the folly of avenging himself and of bearing the guilt of needless bloodshed (v. 31). She showed great insight and intelligence. David listened and acknowledged that she was right (vv. 32–34). Humble and gentle, Abigail helped David learn patience and forbearance. Later on, David married Abigail. The two lived for awhile at Gath and in Hebron, where their son Chileab (or Daniel) was born.

14. Everyone gets angry at times. Anger motivates us

to act to defend ourselves or others and to correct or prevent injustice. Focus the discussion not so much on what makes us angry but rather on our need to control our anger (Ephesians 4:25–26) so that it serves godly, rather than sinful, purposes. The consequences of uncontrolled anger often hurt us more than the original provocation. We may become physically violent and hurt others. We may say damaging things that cannot be retracted. We may injure ourselves physically or emotionally. We may put ourselves in spiritual jeopardy. Anger can make us rash. Not all anger is sinful. God Himself is angry at times. But anger can lead to sin, which we want to avoid. Encourage, but don't press, personal sharing. You can foster trust by sharing examples from your own life.

Day 4 • 1 Samuel 26–28

15. (a) David believed God would right the wrongs Saul had done. Meanwhile, David refused to avenge himself by harming "the LORD's anointed." He knew if he did, he would be guilty too. By God's grace at work in his life, David showed great faith and patience, time after time. Point out that by his restraint David set a good example for Abishai and others who would live under David in his own future kingdom. David demonstrated respect for the authority Saul held and for Saul's office, even though Saul as a person earned no respect by his actions. This set a precedent for those whom David would later rule. (b) Let volunteers comment. By God's grace, we can settle decisions about pornography, violence, respect for authority, and other difficult issues in our minds ahead of time. As the Lord leads us to recall these decisions, He can enable us to walk away from temptations without stopping to consider them. This can be a helpful practice, particularly with especially strong or frequent temptations.

16. Allow participants to share opinions. In a way, David seems worn down, almost desperate for a resolution. He pushes Saul to explain his reasons for hounding him. Who has made Saul so angry at David? Is it God? Is it other people? But even though David seems to be in pain, he speaks in a reasonable way, and he clearly expresses his faith in God's deliverance (vv. 23–24).

17. (a) Let volunteers comment. David faced some hard choices: He could continue running or he could hide outside Saul's territory. He decided to escape to find sanctuary with the Philistines (vv. 2, 6, 7). From there, he attacked, killed, and plundered neighboring nations (v. 9) but not anyone from Israel, not even Saul's tribe, Benjamin, though it lay close to Philistia. David took precautions to ensure that the rulers of the Philistines did not find out the true nature of his raids (vv. 10–12). One might argue that David did Saul's work—protecting God's people from their enemies while Saul obsessed about finding and killing David. Saul could have solidified his people's allegiance and respect by simply doing his job. But envy and rage blind people to the truth. On the other hand, the Philistines were the enemies of God's people. Taking refuge in Philistia hardly seems an act based on faith. Accept responses participants can defend. (b) Don't force anyone to comment, but do accept responses from volunteers. Our Lord would have us act in faith, from strength—His strength, not on fear. His grace will empower us to do this.

18. Saul knew that God had forbidden sorcery. Leviticus makes it clear that all the "black magic arts" amount to cavorting with Satan and his demons. Saul knew this because he himself had outlawed the use of mediums. The Lord had said, "Do not turn to mediums or wizards; do not seek them out, and so make yourselves unclean by them: I am the LORD your God" (Leviticus 19:31). By seeking out the witch of Endor, Saul clearly and knowingly disregarded God's Word. His rebellion was blatant. Sin had turned his heart to granite.

19. Saul rejected God's Word, and God ultimately then rejected Saul. Because Saul was disobedient, David would replace him as king. In 28:16–19, Saul sees a "ghost" and learns that both he and his sons will die in battle the next day. He melts to the ground in fear. At last, Saul seems to grasp the awful consequences of disregarding God's Word.

Day 5 • 1 Samuel 29–31

20. **Challenge question.** God had ordained that David would be king of Israel. What a problem it would have presented if David had been forced to fight against God's own people! God influenced events for good in David's life. God acted sovereignly at a time when David had no way to save himself.

21. (a) Let participants comment. Our culture says, "Real men don't cry; they cope." But David, the "man after God's own heart," expressed open grief and wasn't afraid to show his faith in the Lord openly either. These were signs of strength, not weakness. Jesus Himself wept at the tomb of Lazarus. (b) *For personal reflection. Sharing optional.* We, too, can show our grief when we experi-

ence loss. A "stiff upper lip" isn't necessarily a sign of great faith or strength. Still, we do not grieve "as others do who have no hope" (1 Thessalonians 4:13). Our Lord provides strength and comfort for us as He did for David.

22. Allow volunteers to share opinions. Saul's sad life began with such promise. God gifted him and chose him for leadership. But Saul's tragic flaw was his careless disregard of God's Word and will. Saul failed to listen to God and to obey Him. He cared too much about what others thought of him and too little about God's will. Perhaps most tragically, he failed to repent, even when given ample opportunity.

23. Let volunteers comment. Our Lord is truly gracious. He patiently waits and works with us too, leading us in kindness to repentance. Eventually, His grace comes to an end, but only when we have hardened our hearts beyond repair. This should both warn and comfort us: warn—in the sense that we not despise the grace of God but that we repent quickly when we become aware of sin in our lives; comfort—in the sense that Christ's cross covers all our sins and His grace invites us to come without fear to receive God's forgiveness and help to overcome our sins.

David on the Rise

2 Samuel 1:1–5:5

Preparing for the Session

Central Focus

David resisted shedding the blood of Saul and his kinsmen. Despite this, war breaks out between those in Israel loyal to Saul and those in Judah loyal to David. Nevertheless, David unites the two kingdoms with wisdom and justice.

Objectives

That participants, led by the Holy Spirit working through God's Word, will

1. see how David, the Lord's anointed, is acknowledged as king by Israel and Judah;

2. identify the rivalries in their own lives that could easily escalate into open conflict; and

3. pursue peace and godliness.

For the Small-Group Leader

Small-Group Discussion Helps

Day 1 • 2 Samuel 1

1. The account in 1 Samuel 31 indicates that Saul committed suicide. The young Amalekite, on the other hand, claims he killed Saul. Because he was probably not part of Saul's army, he may have been robbing corpses when he came upon Saul. He may have lied, expecting David to reward him for killing his enemy. Once again, David shows his respect for "the LORD's anointed" (1 Samuel 24:6). He will not raise his own hand against the one God chose, nor will he allow anyone else to show disrespect for God's servant. David took no satisfaction in Saul's death.

2. (a) Three times David cries, "How the mighty have fallen!" Jonathan, and especially Saul as Israel's king, held a place of high honor in David's heart. Despite Saul's despicable deeds, David chose to honor God by honoring the king God set in place. (b) David praises the successes and the good qualities of both men. He expresses no bitterness, and he takes no pleasure in these deaths. David curses the spot where they died. David grieves for Jonathan, his friend and spiritual brother. He gratefully acknowledges Jonathan's exceptional love and loyalty. All these reveal, among other things, that David was a man of great compassion and commitment to the Lord's will for Israel.

3. (a) *For personal reflection. Sharing optional.* It isn't easy to forgive. Only the Spirit working within gives us the power to forgive others as God has forgiven us (Galatians 5:24–26; Ephesians 4:22–32). (b) It is important to resolve conflicts and rivalries quickly, because when bitterness grows, it pollutes and endangers not only those in conflict but others associated with each person as well. Talents are wasted. Whole lifetimes can be misspent and one's health and happiness forfeited. Only by the grace of God in Christ can the Spirit remove jealousy and work the miracle of reconciliation. Christ did this between us and God. His Spirit does this among people. Perhaps group members are willing to tell about a personal youthful rivalry that caused problems or ones that were resolved satisfactorily. (c) Paul recognizes that peace in our relationships does not depend solely on us. Insofar as it is possible, insofar as peace depends on us, we are to live at peace with everyone (Romans 12:18). We cannot keep someone from holding a grudge against us. We can only "pursue what makes for peace" (Romans 14:19), doing whatever we can to promote unity in the Lord. Sometimes that will mean provoking conversation when someone has sinned against us. Living at peace does not mean "playing doormat" for someone who hurts us.

Day 2 • 2 Samuel 2

4. Allow for opinions. Point out that even though David knew God had selected him to rule over all Israel, he refrained from making any move without the Lord's direction. Once again, David asked God what he should do (cf. 1 Samuel 30:7–8), and God answered. David's move to Hebron was part of God's plan. Instead of being headstrong and self-assertive, David was willing to follow God's direction. By faith, David knew that He could trust God. Also, David brought his two wives, each from

a different tribe and region, to live with him in Hebron. He brought his several hundred fighting men and their families to settle there. These loyal citizens might influence the political opinions of others.

5. During his years on the run, David had curried the favor of the rulers in Judah. He restored the livestock and loot stolen by the Philistines and Amalekites. He had shared with them booty from his own raids. He had spared their flocks during his campaigns. In all these ways, David had built up their trust in him.

6. David commends the men of Jabesh-gilead for their tribute to Saul and his family. David is a wise diplomat. He is willing to forgive old wrongs and, by his words, assures Saul's loyal friends that he wants to cultivate their friendship and loyalty now. He never saw himself as Saul's enemy. And he did not see Saul's friends as enemies either.

7. Abner appeared determined that Saul's dynasty should survive—this in spite of David's anointing. Clearly, David is God's choice. Yet, Abner may have personal ambitions for power. Stubbornly, Abner sets up Ish-bosheth as king over the northern tribes of Israel, with intentions to manipulate him. In doing so, Abner sets himself against both God and David—dangerous indeed.

8. Encourage sharing. Point out that David wrote this psalm at a time when Abner opposed him, Israel threatened Judah, and war seemed likely. Yet, David saw in God his *light, salvation, stronghold,* and *help*. David relies on God to *hide* him and *lift [him] high*. David is willing to wait patiently for God to act. Note how God sustains his servant and lifts his spirits (vv. 4–9). Our faithful God will sustain us too. How sure we can be of that as we, with David, wait for the Lord.

9. Bloodshed is seldom the answer to conflict. In this case, a chosen few from each side killed one another. No one survived the test. The dispute remained unsettled. Then a full-scale battle broke out (2:17), and many more lives were lost.

10. In any conflict, one party must be willing to stop, turn around, and listen to the other. Level-headed communication and a desire for the mutual good are essential. Egotism must give way to love and compassion. Sometimes people of the world see the reasonableness of this and are able by sheer force of their will to surrender their ego. Usually, however, conflicts that have escalated to the point of the one between Abner and Joab are resolved only when one or both parties come to faith in Christ. Only the power of the Holy Spirit is strong enough to melt the hatred and spite involved.

Day 3 • 2 Samuel 3:1–21

11. Let participants speculate. David's polygamy would have made life much more difficult in many ways. The enrichment magazine has an article on the affects of David's polygamy. If participants have questions, refer them to it.

12. Abner was insulted and enraged by Ish-bosheth's questions because he saw himself as the real power behind the throne and, as such, above criticism. He turned on Ish-bosheth in favor of David. God used the incident to bring the tribes of Israel under David's rule. God works even through human foibles to advance His purposes.

13. (a) Abner takes the initiative. He proposes an alliance with David. Abner shows that he indeed is the real power behind Ish-bosheth's throne. (b) David insists on Michal's return. This move consolidates his rule by reuniting his household with that of Saul. (c) Abner confers with the elders of Israel. He gets their consensus. (d) David fearlessly meets Abner face-to-face and prepares a "good faith" feast for them.

14. **Challenge question.** David was confident that in His own time God would establish the kingdom and empower him to rule God's people politically and spiritually. David believed this was God's covenant with him and that God would keep His promise. David was not only patient but also willing to let it happen the way God wanted. Other answers are possible; accept those drawn from the text.

Day 4 • 2 Samuel 3:22–39

15. (a) When Joab returned to find that Abner had formed an alliance with David, he was beside himself with rage. His heart filled with hate and a desire for revenge. He had none of David's patient and forgiving spirit. (b) God wants us to repay evil with good and to live in peace. God will punish evil and avenge the wrongs done to His people. He wants us, in kindness and by His grace, to seek to win the offender over. (c) Jesus taught us to turn the other cheek, to be generous, and to love our enemies. He urges us to repay evil with good and to be merciful. (d) *For personal reflection. Sharing optional.* Encourage group members in God's forgiveness and power. His grace will work in our hearts

everything we need to obey Him. We rely on His strength, not our own.

16. David was no stranger to bloodshed. He, too, had taken the lives of hundreds of victims. And Abner had been his rival and foe. But now David's reputation with the people of Israel was at stake. Joab's act made David's overtures to those who had been loyal to King Saul appear hypocritical. The murder put the peace process in jeopardy. Joab's act also revealed his scorn for David; it made David appear weak and unable to control his general. In addition, David genuinely esteemed Abner's leadership ability. David knew that a great man, one of God's gifts to His people, had fallen.

17. David publicly declared his innocence. He cursed Joab's family and declared a national day of mourning. He gave Abner a distinguished burial in Hebron. He fasted and wept publicly.

Day 5 • 2 Samuel 4:1–5:5

18. Perhaps they expected to be rewarded. They surely expected David to rejoice that no more rivals to Israel's throne could arise from Saul's line. (If someone mentions Saul's grandson, Mephibosheth [v. 4], point out that his physical deformity disqualified him in the light of public opinion in that day and time. He was therefore no threat to David.)

19. David quoted the precedent he had set at Saul's death and acknowledged that God had delivered him from all his troubles. He trusted God's action on his behalf and deplored this attempt to engineer events. Then, in justice (v. 12), he enforced the death penalty on the two young men because of their confession to the crime of murder.

20. The representatives of the tribes of Israel (a) declared their kinship with David; (b) acknowledged his military achievements; and (c) expressed their trust in God's choice of David to be their ruler and shepherd.

21. (a) As did Paul in Romans, the writer to the Hebrews urges readers to make every effort to live in peace. It's much easier to quarrel, to compete, and to seek revenge than to communicate, compromise, forgive, and love others as ourselves. Our sinful human nature wars against the Spirit of God who indwells us. But the grace of God extends to all sinners. We can share it instead of hoarding it. Finally, says the writer to the Hebrews, jealousy and rivalry feed on selfishness and self-centeredness. Like a bitter root, these grow to poison many people and relationships. (b) *For personal reflection. Sharing optional.* You could work together to list ways to actively pursue peace as God's Spirit empowers you—to be proactive in the peace process at home, work, school, church; to pray for one another, especially that the power of the Holy Spirit would be active in your hearts, minds, and lives; and so on. Accept responses and comments drawn from the texts included in this week's study.

Small-Group Leaders Session 5 — **Life of David**

David on the Throne

2 Samuel 5:6–10:19

Preparing for the Session

Central Focus

David consolidates the kingdom and conquers neighboring enemies. In one case, he overpowers a mighty stronghold called Jerusalem and makes it his capital. He plans to build a temple for the Lord, but the Lord promises something better: an eternal dynasty for David's Greater Son.

Objectives

That participants, led by the Holy Spirit working through God's Word, will

1. recognize David's God-given political, military, and diplomatic skills in building the nation of Israel;

2. review God's promise to David and its fulfillment in Christ; and

3. rely more fully on God's promises in their Baptism.

For the Small-Group Leader

Small-Group Discussion Helps

Day 1 • 2 Samuel 5:6–25

1. David's capture of Jerusalem was significant for several reasons. The city, an unconquered Canaanite stronghold, did not belong to either Judah or Israel, yet was strategically located near the boundary of both. By taking it, David now could weld both quarreling groups into one nation. In capturing the city, David also showed his expert military strategy; his victory sent a signal to surrounding nations that Israel was now a power to be reckoned with. The Lord was with David; no enemy could stand against him and his people.

2. David knew that God had made him king. His reign was to fulfill God's purposes for His people. David realized that he ruled at the pleasure of God to serve His people.

3. (a) Moses gave clear guidance concerning Israel's selection of a king. David was surely God's choice and a fellow Israelite. (b) However, David's polygamy was a direct disobedience to God's ordinance. Had David followed the law God laid down in Deuteronomy 17:18–19; had he copied, studied, and reviewed God's Law, his family and his kingdom could have turned out differently. Perhaps David succumbed to the values of his times (e.g., the Middle East cultures of that time judged a man's prestige by the number of wives and children he could boast about). David's polygamy would bring him enormous pain and humiliation. And it would damage the kingdom.

4. David could face his enemies with confidence because he first asked God to guide him (v. 19). When he was successful, he credited God with the victory (v. 20). Encourage participants to share times the Lord has directed them and made victory possible in their own lives. Discuss the importance of knowing God's Word as we seek His guidance. Also stress our need for the Spirit's power to comply quickly and quietly to the Lord's direction. Also stress God's willingness to forgive us for Christ's sake when we fail, as we all will at times.

Day 2 • 2 Samuel 6:1–23

5. By bringing the ark to Jerusalem, David emphasized the preeminent importance of God's presence in the national life of His people. For many years, Israel had neglected her spiritual life. Saul certainly had set no example of piety or obedience. The ark was almost forgotten, the priesthood had been nearly killed off, and the people were becoming more pagan. The ark symbolized the presence of God and His covenant promises, particularly the promise to send the Savior. The Mercy Seat was the place where God and sinners met, where God removed their sin on the Day of Atonement. The Mercy Seat looked forward to the cross and served as a reminder of what the Savior would do there. By bringing the ark to Jerusalem, David acknowledged God's rule over both himself and the entire nation.

6. (a) The ark was holy. The elaborate instructions were given so no one violated the holiness by contacting it in any way. (b) The Lord designated one group of priests to carry the ark by slipping long poles through rings

located on the sides. (c) Scripture nowhere mentions an ox cart as a means by which the ark could be transported. (d) With no doubt the best intentions, Uzzah tried to steady the ark, to keep it from falling. But his act was one of irreverence and disobedience. He died for it! "Meaning well" while nonetheless disobeying God counts for nothing. A holy God expects full and complete obedience. God intended this incident to teach this truth. However, nothing in the account would lead us to believe Uzzah lost his salvation with this sin. In all likelihood, we will meet him in heaven.

7. (a) David had gone to a great deal of trouble to prepare for the celebration (1 Chronicles 15). He had offered sacrifices for his own sins and for the sins of his people (2 Samuel 6:13). His joy in the Lord's greatness and mercy exhilarated him. Dressed not as a king in kingly robes, but simply, as the Levites were, David enthusiastically expressed his thanks and humility before the Lord. Michal could not understand all this. She stayed home and refused to take part. Perhaps she did not share David's love for God. Perhaps she compared his actions with what she remembered of those of the royal court of her father, King Saul. David returned from the celebration jubilant and ready to bless his family as he'd blessed his people. But Michal met him with selfish, biting sarcasm. Apparently, the couple remained estranged from that time on. (b) David had determined years before to trust God's election of him as Israel's king. By God's grace, he was willing to be a humble servant of his God (vv. 21–22). Not even his own wife's criticism would deter him.

Day 3 • 2 Samuel 7

8. David wanted to build a house for the Lord. The ark of the covenant rested in a tent in Jerusalem, while David lived in a palace (5:9–11). This apparently didn't seem right to David. At this time, David was at "rest" (v. 1). All his enemies had been subdued, and he had time to think more about God's honor. Also, the ark of the covenant was now in Jerusalem as a reminder of God's presence. David no doubt wanted to honor the God who had done so much and whose presence had meant so much to him during his prior fifteen years of struggle.

9. Accept volunteers' comments. Answers will vary.

10. **Challenge question.** God would allow David's family to provide the royal lineage for the Greater David, Jesus the Messiah. The prophets foretold this; the evangelists witnessed its fulfillment; and the apostles spread the Good News. Accept specific promises drawn from the wording of the five texts in the study leaflet question.

11. (a) Let volunteers comment. David could have felt rebuffed. After all, God's prophet Nathan had at first encouraged David's plan to build a temple for God. Yet, David does not argue or complain. This powerful man sits before God in humble, quiet, submissive, respectful reverence. He accepts God's will. He acknowledges his own unworthiness. Seven times David calls God "O Lord God." The Lord God Almighty is King David's King. He praises God for who He is and what He's done. (b) David asks God to keep His promise (v. 25). David knows he can trust God's Word (v. 28). He asks God to bless him and his descendants as He has promised (v. 29).

12. Take time to share insights. Involve everyone in this discussion. Guide participants to see these points:

• Those who belong to the Lord submit to His timing and His good and gracious will because they trust His love for them.

• God is good to us—not because we are sinless or faithful; we are not—but because He is a loving God. He remains true to His Word and always has our best interests at heart.

• God planned our salvation in eternity; He works in time through weak and sinful human beings to accomplish His purposes.

• God chose us in love to become His adopted sons and daughters. Even though God knows us completely, He still wants us to be His own and has chosen us for special service to Him.

• We can be utterly confident that God will keep His promises to us. He kept His promise to send Jesus, our Savior. We can rely on Him to meet all our other needs as well.

Day 4 • 2 Samuel 8–9

13. David was not only a highly successful military leader but he was also a wise monarch who ruled his people in justice. He seems uncorrupted by the wealth he gained from plundering those he vanquished; he dedicated most of it to the Lord, contributing much of it to the temple building fund. He had great worldly power, but he had learned during his years in the wilderness to trust the Lord, not his own wisdom or strength. He gave God the glory for what he accomplished.

14. Like Mephibosheth, we were poor and far off, hopeless and helpless, children of Satan, the true King's sworn enemy. But our King Jesus searched for us, found us, and graciously invited us into His own household. We, too, are adopted into God's family as royal sons and daughters, and we share His bounty, all the riches of the heavenly home.

Day 5 • 2 Samuel 10:1–19

15. The new ruler of Ammon, Hanun, humiliated a delegation of David's men who came to offer David's sympathy on the death of Hanun's father.

16. Let volunteers comment. The magnitude of David's victory against what must have been overwhelming enemy forces can be demonstrated by several examples in this chapter.

17. (a) By God's grace, David trusted God's Word. He wasn't corrupted by wealth, but he honored God with his gifts and in his life. He praised and worshiped God. He showed kindness to others in response to God's kindness to him. (b) David ruled his people with justice. He sought God's direction. He organized the administration of the kingdom. He accepted God's plans for him. He learned from his mistakes. He credited God for his success. (c) David was unpretentious and joined his people in praising God. He related to the people, gave them gifts, and blessed them. He won victory after victory and raised Israel's prestige among nations. (d) David's righteous attitudes were gifts of God, not things that David drummed up inside himself. The victories David won came also as God's gifts to David and to his people. Throughout Scripture, we see God acting on behalf of those He has chosen. He—only and always—is our Hero and the true Hero of all the Scriptures.

Small-Group Leaders Session 6

Life of David

David on the Edge

2 Samuel 11–12

Preparing for the Session

Central Focus

David had acquired many treasures, wives and lands, but it was apparently not enough for his sinful nature. His lust gave way to adultery and murder. The prophet Nathan skillfully exposed David's guilt by applying God's Law. David repented, whereupon he found a gracious Lord who both forgave him and helped him face the consequences of his sin.

Objectives

That participants, led by the Holy Spirit working through God's Word, will

1. understand how David, in despising God's Word despised the Lord Himself;

2. begin to appreciate the terrible consequences of sin; and

3. acknowledge their own sins and receive God's forgiveness through grace in Christ.

For the Small-Group Leader

Small-Group Discussion Helps

Day 1 • 2 Samuel 11:1–13

1. (a) Let participants comment. David failed to pay close attention to God's Word. The Law specifically said Israel's king should not take multiple wives (Deuteronomy 17:17). David ignored this. God gave specific instructions on transporting the ark (Numbers 4:5–20; 7:1–9). David did not pay attention. We can't tell whether David was ignorant, careless, or defiant, but the result was the same—trouble for himself and others. His willful self-indulgence would later result in near disaster. (b) David apparently gave in to self-indulgence. The Law was clear about adultery (Exodus 20:14). David defied God's specific law.

2. (a) David should have been on the battlefield (v.1). Perhaps he was feeling old or tired. Perhaps he was becoming accustomed to a softer life in a lavish royal court. With little to do, David was perhaps bored. Satan always sees to it that temptations come to us when we are most vulnerable. Bathsheba's beauty tempted David. He didn't look away. Instead, he let his heart fill with lust until he was out of control. (b) Lust surely played a part. Yet, there was more at the heart of David's sin. David usurped God's place and made himself judge of what was best for him. What David wants, David will have. This is, of course, a sin against the First Commandment. Whenever we violate one of the other nine commandments, we also violate the First.

3. Uriah was a Hittite, not an Israelite. He may have adopted the Israelite faith, because *Uriah* means "my light is the LORD." His loyalty to Israel, to David, and to his fellow officers is remarkable. His sense of fairness and his selflessness contrast sharply with David's self-indulgence in this account. From 2 Samuel 23:39, we see that Uriah was part of David's select bodyguard.

4. (a) God had chosen and gifted David. God had loved, guided, protected, and honored David. By his sin, David showed that he despised all this. David's concern about the honor of God's name, His reputation among the pagans, doesn't seem to matter anymore. (b) As if that were not enough, David wronged Bathsheba. Before this incident, it seems he didn't even know her (2 Samuel 11:13). Now he depersonalized her and used her for his own gratification. It's debatable whether she could have refused to come when David sent for her. He was, after all, the king.

5. We cannot fight off the powerful pull of sin on our own. We need to use the power of God's Word (Psalm 119:11) as we encounter temptations. As Paul points out in his letter to the Galatians (5:16–25), living by the prompting and power of the Spirit is the key to conquering sinful desires. Belonging to Christ by faith, we receive the power of the Holy Spirit as He works in us through Word and Sacrament. Those who are in Christ will stay close to Him through these Means of Grace. The Spirit, ever active in His Word, will work His way in our hearts.

Until the day we go home to be with Jesus, we will sin; perfection is not possible this side of heaven. But as we confess our sins and receive God's pardon, He works in us to produce more godly desires and Christlike character. As a practical matter, 2 Timothy 2:22 urges us to run away from temptations, particularly temptations of the flesh. James 4:7 encourages us to submit to God and urges us to resist Satan—all this by the power of the Spirit.

Day 2 • 2 Samuel 11:14–27

6. (a) The punishment for adultery was death. (b) David knew the consequences for adultery. Bathsheba's pregnancy would testify to David's sin. David decided there was no way to escape except to kill Uriah and marry Bathsheba. So he plotted what we might call a governmental cover-up to save himself.

7. Allow for opinions. Encourage participants to give reasons for their answers. By his sin, David drew Joab into his murderous plot; he turned on a loyal soldier—one of his own bodyguards; he exploited Bathsheba; he murdered an innocent man; he stole another man's wife; he carelessly endangered other lives in his army by unnecessarily exposing them to the enemy in battle. David's deceit and hypocrisy and his bringing dishonor on his nation were all despicable. Worst of all, David had brought blasphemy on God's name among the heathen (2 Samuel 12:14).

8. Bathsheba utters not a word in our text. We know she was beautiful and that she submitted to David's summons. She mourned Uriah's death and later the death of her child (2 Samuel 12:24). Whatever her attitude and motives, David is clearly the one whom God held responsible, but they both suffered.

9. Spend some time sharing answers to this question. Point out the obvious: God hates sin. He is holy. His children are to be reflections of Himself (1 Peter 1:16). Sin is a betrayal of God's image. It perverts and twists and injures the relationship between God and His child. Sin is rebellion, a rejection of the plans God has for His child. God knows the effects of sin—suffering, death, and brokenness. God would spare His child all this. That's why our sin displeases Him so very much.

Day 3 • 2 Samuel 12:1–14

10. (a) The Word of God is dynamic, living, and active in accomplishing His purposes. It is sharper than a double-edged sword, because it can penetrate to the heart of a person, revealing thoughts and attitudes hidden there. (b) God's Word, spoken through Nathan the prophet, penetrated David's innermost being, laying bare his sin and guilt, accomplishing God's purpose, namely, leading him to admit his transgression.

11. Encourage participants to share what God said to David through Nathan. Responses may include words like this: "I chose you to be king. I delivered you from your enemies. I gave you Saul's throne and all he owned. I gave you the nations of Israel and Judah. Yet, I would have given you more. You despised My Word. You despised Me. You did what was evil. You killed Uriah and took Bathsheba."

12. The Holy Spirit led David to confess, "I have sinned against the LORD." The Spirit was still at work within David, showing him his sin and causing him to cast himself totally on God's mercy, to trust God's forgiveness.

13. *For personal reflection. Sharing optional.* Don't discuss your specific answers. But do talk about the process of confession and its benefits. Confessing is a vital part of the Christian life. While we need not agonize, torturing ourselves in an attempt to recall each and every fault, refusal to confess known sin puts us in a dangerous position. It can eventually lead us to harden our hearts and to lose our faith. When we sin against someone, in addition to going to God, we may need also to go to the one we have wronged and ask for forgiveness. As discussion winds down, recite the words of 1 John 1:8–9 together: "If we say we have no sin, we deceive ourselves, and the truth is not in us. If we confess our sins, He is faithful and just to forgive us our sins and to cleanse us from all unrighteousness." Also remind your group of the availability and power of private confession. Martin Luther commented that strong Christians might not need to use this tool in their spiritual lives, but he did not count himself among those who were strong enough to live without it. No one should be forced to confess to the pastor. We confess our sins not as a good work whereby we gain favor with God or make up for our sins, but rather because of the great comfort and hope God gives us through the words of Absolution: *Your sins are forgiven.* That comfort gives us power in our battle against temptation and Satan's schemes.

14. We do not know exactly when David composed Psalm 51. We do know from the superscription that the adultery with Bathsheba precipitated the composition. He may have written it immediately after Nathan's confrontation or after several months had passed—months of thought and reflection. The spirit of the entire psalm is reflected in David's confession to Nathan in 2 Samuel 12:13: "I have sinned against the LORD." (a) David ad-

mits to transgression (defiant rebellion), iniquity (perverse wickedness), and sin (moral failure) in verses 1–2. Over and over, David admits to being sinful and to his transgressions (vv. 3–5, 9). David knows that sin will separate him from God (v. 11). He pleads that God blot out his sin, wash him, and cleanse him (vv. 1–2, 7). (b) David takes responsibility for his sin: "*my* sin", "*my* transgressions", "*I* sinned", "*I* was brought forth in iniquity" (vv. 3–5). Painful pleading echoes throughout the first half of the psalm. (c) In verses 8–12, David declares his confidence in God's mercy and his hope for restoration: "Let me hear joy and gladness; let the bones that You have broken rejoice" (v. 8). "Restore to me the joy of Your salvation" (v. 12). (d) In response to God's gracious forgiveness, David promises to witness to others (v. 13), leading them to repentance too. His "tongue will sing aloud of [God's] righteousness" (v. 14) and "[his] mouth will declare [God's] praise" (v. 15). He offers God the "sacrifices" of his broken and contrite heart (v. 17). (e) Let volunteers comment. Some group members may have memorized parts of this psalm already. Perhaps some use this psalm as a prayer before Holy Communion. Ask for other thoughts and ideas.

Day 4 • 2 Samuel 12:15–25

15. The child born to Bathsheba and David died. (b) **Challenge question.** The pagan peoples who heard about David's crimes might conclude that the God of Israel winked at the sin of Israel's leaders or that He did not take sins seriously. Because David held such a public position of leadership, the Lord may have found it necessary to do what He did. Even in the death of the child, though, we see God's mercy. In one sense, the child died instead of David—thus foreshadowing the sacrifice of David's "son," the Messiah who became the eternal king on David's throne. Also point out (v. 23) David's faith that his infant son was with the Lord in eternity. The child could want no better life than life in the throne room of heaven itself.

16. Although he pleads with God for his child, David accepts God's handling of his case. His grief is deep and painful, yet he does not despair. He trusts God's forgiveness and wisdom (v. 20), and so he gets up and goes on with life. David realizes God has acted. Nothing can change what has happened. Yet, David expresses his faith in a reunion with his son in eternity (v. 23). He knows he has been redeemed. David is right with God again. He goes to the house of his God to worship Him. David and God are at peace.

17. With renewed spiritual strength, David is able to comfort his wife. David, now reunited with God, can experience a oneness with Bathsheba the two had not experienced before. The new life they conceived holds promise for their future. But the greatest sign that David is fully restored is God's declaration that He loves their child. *Jedidiah* means "Beloved of the Lord." What encouragement in this message from God's spokesman.

Day 5 • 2 Samuel 12:26–31

18. God granted victory on the battlefield.

19. This question makes two specific applications of the lesson events to our lives. (a) Our need for God's grace is the same in times of prosperity as well as in times of turmoil. That grace is our only real defense against temptation, no matter what our outward circumstances. (b) This incident brings out the incredible grace of God. He forgives *all* sin, sins against the Fifth and Sixth Commandments included. Help participants realize and express this.

Small-Group Leaders Session 7

Life of David

David under the Sword

2 Samuel 13:1–22:51

Preparing for the Session

Central Focus

The consequences of David's sin produce havoc in his life. The members of his own household become his enemies. His kingdom lies on the verge of splitting apart. Those whom he had formerly conquered now rise again with menacing threats. In it all, David trusts the Lord to be his rock, fortress, and salvation.

Objectives

That participants, led by the Holy Spirit working through God's Word, will

1. witness the disintegration of relationships in David's household;

2. acknowledge the consequences of sin in their own personal relationships; and

3. rely on the Lord and His promises in the midst of personal trauma.

For the Small-Group Leader

Small-Group Discussion Helps

Day 1 • 2 Samuel 13:1–15:12

1. (a) By this time, David had nineteen sons and one daughter by his many wives (1 Chronicles 3:1–9). He also had had children by his concubines. Clearly, these multiple relationships became hotbeds for jealousy and rivalry. How much of their father's attention did David's children enjoy? How effectively could he shape his children's faith and their values? (Some of his wives were either pagan or seemingly indifferent to David's God.) Specifically in 2 Samuel 13, we read that Amnon, David's firstborn and heir apparent to David's throne, raped his half-sister, Tamar. He vented his lust, hate, and abuse on this innocent victim. Tamar is ruined and driven to despair. Absalom, another of David's sons and Tamar's full brother, was outraged and vindictive. So Absalom murdered Amnon, and he despised his father for failing to take appropriate action against Amnon. No doubt the murder was wrong; even so, Absalom's outrage was justified. (b) Spend some time discussing David's role as a parent. He seems indulgent (13:7), perhaps naive, and preoccupied. Even though he is angry (13:21), he seems unrealistic about the seriousness both of Amnon's sin and of the breach that has developed between Amnon and Absalom. David fails to discipline Amnon, adding fuel to Absalom's rage. David ignores Tamar's suffering. He mourns for his sons (13:36, 39), yet fails to deal promptly with Absalom's sin, letting him flee to his grandfather's home in Geshur. David neglected to correct his children and to ground them in the faith of Israel. His priorities lie in disarray (Deuteronomy 6:1–15). (c) Trouble is no stranger even in Christian families. Encourage participants to suggest reasons. At the heart of such trouble may be a lack of unifying faith and commitment to God and one another; a lack of living together in repentance, forgiveness, and love; a lack of parental responsibility to model and teach the life in Christ Jesus. Be careful, though, how you phrase this. Adam and Eve had the only perfect Parent, and they fell into sin and rebellion (Genesis 3). Since then, all parents have been sinners; no parent does everything right. Grown children are responsible before God for their own actions and for the state of their hearts and lives before God. Reassure one another that God's forgiveness, guidance, and power are available for all who trust in Jesus, the Savior.

2. (a) Grief and bitterness keep festering in David's family. Father and son are estranged. Yet, neither makes a move. There's no attempt to face facts, to admit where they've gone wrong, or to ask for each other's forgiveness. Even when Joab succeeds in getting Absalom home again, David refuses to speak to him. It takes David five years (!) after Amnon's murder to come face-to-face with Absalom. Even then, the outward signs of reconciliation—bowing down, kissing—fail to reflect genuine love and respect. (b) Talk about the importance of dealing with problems promptly, communicating effectively and fairly, showing mutual respect, being willing to admit wrongs, and the power God gives us to forgive one another freely and fully. All these are important whether or not the family includes children.

3. Encourage members to share their impressions. To this point, Absalom has shown himself to be calculating, vengeful, violent, deceptive, manipulative, vain, and self-absorbed. A self-appointed mediator of justice, he curries the favor of those seeking retribution. How cleverly he greets them and listens to them, bowing, touching, kissing, and stealing the hearts of the people away from his own father and king. How cleverly he deceives David, gathers supporters, and spirits away Ahithophel, one of David's trusted counselors. Absalom is the consummate politician—with fangs.

Day 2 • 2 Samuel 15:13–18:33 and Psalm 37

4. How ironic that this mighty warrior, slayer of Goliath, victor over "tens of thousands," should so quickly give up and flee Jerusalem under Absalom's threat. David left ten concubines behind to tend the palace. Yet these women, in their position, were virtually powerless and later became victims themselves.

5. David's new faithful friend and warrior Ittai pledged his help. He insisted on remaining with David wherever he went. David convinced Zadok and Abiathar, two loyal priests, to remain in Jerusalem with the ark of the Lord. David wanted it to remain in its place of honor in the royal city. The priests could serve as underground agents and their sons as couriers. Hushai would feign loyalty to Absalom and inform the priests of the traitors' plans. As further reading indicates (2 Samuel 16–17), Hushai would neutralize the advice Ahithophel offered Absalom. Because of Hushai's crucial role, the insurrection would be crushed in a matter of days and a prolonged civil war averted.

6. What a terrible time for David! He is politically, personally, and spiritually under attack. By the outward acts of repentance noted in the study leaflet, he admits openly to God and to other people that he has failed as a leader and father. He is willing to accept God's verdict. He acknowledges that his life, his future, is in God's hands (2 Samuel 15:25–26). His humility and his readiness to repent encourage us in our own times of personal crisis. Talk about the futility of recrimination and bitterness and about the danger of despair at such times. Emphasize the importance of knowing God, being close to Him in His Word, and trusting His love. God gifted David with friends and supporters; He does this for us also in our times of crisis. David was not too proud or stubborn to lean on them. Neither need we be.

7. As David heads down into the Jordan Valley outside Jerusalem, he encounters Shimei's fierce abuse. Showering David with stones, dirt, and curses, Shimei vents a deep and bitter grudge against David. Shimei was convinced David was finished and took great delight in his downfall. David wouldn't allow Abishai to retaliate. He accepts the abuse as possibly accomplishing a part of God's purpose. David was willing to await the outcome of his ordeal patiently. In Psalm 37, David expresses a profound trust in God's goodness: God listens, answers prayer, sends help, and blesses the efforts of His faithful. David would not fret; he would be still and wait for God to act. What amazing faith David had! A true gift of God, who creates and sustains faith in the hearts of His people through His Word!

8. As a way of proclaiming himself supreme monarch, Absalom possesses what is left of David's harem in full public view; he has sex with the ten concubines David had left behind to tend the palace (vv. 20–21). Note that Ahithophel was Bathsheba's grandfather. Perhaps he gave the advice he did out of a desire for revenge.

9. Hushai (working undercover for David) paints a dramatic picture—a huge army, with Absalom in the lead, completely devastating David and his men. This appeals to Absalom! But he will have to break off his pursuit of David in order to amass this army. God answered David's prayer (2 Samuel 15:31) and frustrated Ahithophel's wise advice that Absalom make a quick end to David's party. Because Absalom fails to strike at once, David and his allies are able to cross the river to safety. In the time it would take Absalom to assemble a huge army, David also would assemble his own. Note the various people God used in a variety of ways to assist in David's rescue.

10. Allow participants to evaluate Joab's role in chapter 18. Joab, Ittai, and Abishai, David's three commanders, understood David's clear command concerning Absalom (2 Samuel 18:5). But Joab's intentions are not consistent with David's. In fact, Joab may have secretly offered a bribe to anyone who killed Absalom in battle (v. 11). Joab himself does not hesitate; when he has the opportunity, he kills Absalom. He takes the initiative (v. 16) to announce the end of the conflict and (v. 17) contemptuously flings Absalom's corpse into a hole. He chooses someone he deems expendable, a foreign slave, a Cushite, to take David the news. We don't know Joab's motives. Allow time for discussion.

11. Every parent might well empathize with David in his grief. Talk about the regret he may have felt about

his own role as a father—his failure to correct and discipline his children and to provide a model for them in his own life. David, like many parents, may have been willing to *die* to save his son—yet he was unwilling to *live* for his son while he had a chance. Talk about the love parents have for wayward children. How much more love the heavenly Father had for His wayward human children. He sent Jesus to live and to die for us.

Day 3 • 2 Samuel 19–20

12. David and his family cross the Jordan River, this time on an elaborate ferry that takes them back home. (a) Shimei is first to meet them. David graciously forgives him and spares his life—this time. (b) Ziba and Mephibosheth also meet David, one accusing the other, falling all over themselves to explain their behavior. David cuts their explanation short and tells them to divide Saul's estate. (c) In contrast, David tries to reward his unselfishly loyal subjects, such as the faithful Barzillai, who had helped David through his ordeal (2 Samuel 17:27–29). How much of human nature is revealed in this account!

13. (a) To secure the allegiance of the people of Judah, David replaced Joab (an Israelite) with Amasa (a Judahite). David then sent Amasa on the initiative to attack and destroy the troublemaker Sheba. (b) Joab deliberately murders Amasa and takes the lead once again. Then he pursues Sheba to the fortified city of Abel.

14. Some may recognize Joab's decisive, albeit brutal, action as critical in putting down Sheba's revolt. Joab also shows cunning and determination in building the ramp to the top of the city wall (2 Samuel 20:15). He had the sense to listen to the woman's proposal and to strike a bargain with her (2 Samuel 20:17–21). Others may favor the woman of Abel, who like Abigail (1 Samuel 25:23–31) pleaded for her family/community. Confidently, the woman of Abel promised and produced the head of Sheba. The revolt was ended. Her town was saved.

15. (a) St. Paul urges Christians to serve one another in love, loving our neighbors as ourselves (Galatians 5:14). Led by the Spirit and empowered by the love of Jesus for us, we can be loving, joyful, peaceful, patient, kind, good, faithful, and gentle with one another. By the power of the Spirit, we can put the welfare of others first. (b) Not in our own power or strength, not as a result of our own determination or resolution, but only by the power of the Spirit, alive in us through Word and Sacrament, will we "walk by the Spirit" (Galatians 5:25). The indwelling Holy Spirit, given to us in Baptism, will produce faith and its "fruit" in our lives. We remember the new identity we have received; according to Galatians 3:26 we are "sons" and thus heirs of God. We're free in Christ to love. Our new identity carries with it power to live out the freedom we have been given.

Day 4 • 2 Samuel 21

16. Saul's betrayal of Joshua's oath to the Gibeonites not to destroy them brought about Israel's suffering. The nation understood their three-year famine as a sign of God's anger over Saul's sin. Even though the Gibeonites had won Joshua's pledge by deception (Joshua 9:3–4; 14–15), God held Israel responsible to keep their word, their oath (Joshua 9:18–21).

17. (a) Saul's family would pay the price for his sin. Two sons of his concubine, Rizpah, and five sons of Saul's oldest daughter Merab and her husband, Adriel, would be put to death. Blood for blood. Merab had apparently died early in life, and Michal, David's first wife and Saul's younger daughter, had taken Merab's boys to raise. The young men were killed in public view. This act nearly wiped out the house of Saul. Subsequently, Scripture mentions only the descendants of Jonathan. (b) The heathen cultures all around Israel exacted "justice" from the families of criminals. Children died for their parents' misdeeds; fathers were held responsible for the crimes of their adult sons and daughters. The Lord, the God of Israel, had set a different precedent, though. Each person was to bear his or her own guilt (Deuteronomy 24:16; Ezekiel 18:20). Led by David, Israel apparently violated a clear teaching of Scripture to correct or atone for Saul's murder of the Gibeonites. This was a literal case of "two wrongs don't make a right." Some participants may wonder why God did not censure David for this unholy act of revenge. Perhaps the Lord did reprimand David but chose not to record it. We simply don't know.

18. (a) Both parents mourned the loss of beloved sons. Both refused to be comforted. Perhaps Rizpah's grief aroused David's compassion so that he finally gave her sons a decent burial. Rizpah's devotion touches the heart. She and her family suffered the consequences of Saul's sin. How true also today that often family members endure many hardships because of the sins of others in the family. (b) Verse 14 says nothing about the murder of Saul's seven sons being the reason the famine ended. The verse simply says that God heard the prayers

of His people for their land. As we read the Old Testament, we need to read with care. The Lord did not sanction everything His people did. He didn't approve of everything that was done in His name. God's sending rain and ending the famine proves that His is gracious, not that the deaths of Saul's seven sons pleased Him.

19. David's men were loyal and protective. They recognized that all Israel depended on David for security and recognition as a nation.

Day 5 • 2 Samuel 22 and Psalm 18

20. Note that Psalm 18 is almost identical to the text of 2 Samuel 22. (a) David's metaphors for God include rock, fortress, deliverer (v. 2); shield, horn of salvation, stronghold, refuge, savior (v. 3); Most High (v. 14); my lamp (v. 29); and shield, rock, and salvation (vv. 31, 32, 47). Given David's life experiences, it's not surprising he sees God as his rock—the safe refuge when enemies attack; his shield—for protection in battle; his Savior—from sin and eternal death. (b) God saved David from violence (v. 3) and from enemies (v. 4). God reached down, took hold, and drew David up from the deep (v. 17). God rescued and supported David (vv. 18-20). God turned darkness into light (v. 29); armed David with strength, guided, and equipped him (vv. 33-34, 40); trained him for battle, and gave him victory and honor (vv. 35, 36, 40). God also made David's way sure (v. 37); delivered, preserved, and avenged him (vv. 44-48) and set him free (v. 49). Verse 51 sums up all God has done for David. (c) David recognizes that by God's power he is able to advance against troops and scale walls (v. 30); pursue, crush and utterly destroy his enemies (vv. 38, 41-43); and praise the Lord among the nations, singing God's praises forever (v. 50).

21. Encourage sharing on (a), (b), and (c). Help participants step into David's shoes. We live in a totally different culture and time, but we face many of the same pitfalls David faced. Our sinful nature closely resembles that of David. Remind one another of God's bountiful grace, His unfailing love and readiness to forgive. God is our Rock, our Fortress, and our Savior too. By His power, we can "leap over [the] wall" we face and sing His praise forever.

22. God showed His steadfast love by sending His own Son, Jesus Christ (also David's "son" or descendant) to rescue sinners (2 Samuel 7:8-16). God promised that David's dynasty would endure forever. The promise was fulfilled in the eternal reign of Christ. See also Psalm 89:19-29; John 12:34; Matthew 1:1; Mark 1:11. Session 9 will deal with this in more depth.

Small-Group Leaders Session 8 | **Life of David**

David at the Last

2 Samuel 23–1 Kings 2

Preparing for the Session

Central Focus

Before David "rests with his fathers" and is buried, he again invokes God's wrath and suffers at the hand of his son Adonijah. David succeeds, however, in establishing Solomon on the throne and advises him to observe what the Lord requires.

Objectives

That participants, led by the Holy Spirit working through God's Word, will

1. watch David struggle with temptation and sin until his life's end;

2. rely on the trustworthiness of God to forgive the penitent; and

3. encourage one another to gladly hear God's Word and rely on it for power to overcome temptation.

For the Small-Group Leader

Small-Group Discussion Helps

Day 1 • 2 Samuel 23

1. (a) An oracle is a revelation from God. In this, his final poem or psalm, David announced truths revealed to him by God. David acknowledged his role as prophet (vv. 1–3), someone who proclaimed God's Word in the inspired Scripture he wrote. He also identified himself as the son of Jesse, as the anointed (chosen) one, as one raised on high (exalted) by God, and as the sweet psalmist (singer) of Israel. (b) David describes the perfectly righteous reign of the coming King, Jesus Christ, King David's Greater Son. He is the light of the world, who brings life and salvation. (c) David trusts God's covenant promise. He believed his dynasty ("house") would endure and that through his lineage a Savior would come—a "Greater David" who would complete the work of salvation. (d) We, too, belong to God's "house," as living stones in that "house," the Church made up of all believers in Jesus, "great David's greater Son" (*LSB* 398). (e) David writes that those who reject the coming Righteous King will be destroyed.

2. David respected and loved his warriors. He risked his life for them, standing shoulder to shoulder with them in combat. He shared their hardships and knew many of them by name. In the event recorded in verses 13–17, David was so touched by their devotion and the risk they took for him that he poured out the precious water as an act of worship to his Lord. David felt too unworthy to drink it himself. David saw his men as God's gifts to him.

Day 2 • 2 Samuel 24 and 1 Chronicles 21

3. As 1 Chronicles 21:1 states, Satan was permitted to tempt David. God does not cause anyone to sin (James 1:13–15). David had a clear choice. (a) Taking a census was not in itself evil, but the motivation for the census could be. We can infer from 2 Samuel 24:9 that the census focused mainly on men capable of military service. Perhaps David wanted to know the strength of his army, relying on it instead of trusting in the Lord to defend His people, as Psalm 20:7 urges. (b) When the Holy Spirit convicted David of his sin, he admitted it freely, asked for forgiveness, and trusted in God's mercy (2 Samuel 24:10, 14, 17). Even though he was the king, he remained teachable. He listened to the prophet Gad. (c) *For personal reflection. Sharing optional.* We know God forgives us not because we feel it but because He has promised that in His Word. He assures us of it in the Sacrament of the Altar in the words "given and shed for you for the forgiveness of sin." Encourage one another to rely on the trustworthiness of God to forgive the penitent.

4. **Challenge question.** (a) The text (2 Samuel 24:1) says that God was angry with *Israel*. (b) The plague did not come as revenge or as a "payback" for sin. God punished Jesus for Israel's sins (and for ours); He does not punish us. Instead, the plague was intended to bring Israel to repentance for the sins of pride and self-reliance (idolatry) they had committed. (c) Jesus took all our punishment in our place on the cross. In exchange, we receive His right-standing with God. In this, Jesus did

much, much more for us than David did for his people. Even now, our Lord Jesus is interceding for us.

5. (a) God told David to build an altar on Araunah's threshing floor. There, David would offer an appropriate sacrifice as a sin offering for himself and for his people. God Himself appointed this altar and the sacrifice—in the very same place that Abraham had built an altar and had laid his son Isaac on it as a sacrifice. On that same spot, Solomon would build God's temple, and its altars would hold the sacrifices He had prescribed, sacrifices that would remind the people of the one, final, perfect sacrifice to come on Calvary. All these "altars" were signs of peace and reconciliation between sinful people and a holy God. (b) David knew God. This lifelong relationship had taught him he could trust God completely. David was candid, ready to admit when he was wrong, confident of God's wisdom and mercy. Even though he stumbled, David wanted to do God's will and worship Him aright. (c) David refused to offer something that cost him nothing. His love for the Lord was such that he wanted to honor Him by giving his very best. Our gifts of money to God honor Him too. He does not need our dollars, but we give them as a sign that we have first given Him ourselves—our whole being.

Day 3 • 1 Kings 1

6. The first verses of 1 Kings indicate how old age had slowed David. He needed care. We might conclude he took a less active role in the administration of the kingdom. David didn't seem to notice Adonijah imitating Absalom, setting himself up as David's successor (v. 6). Adonijah won the support of Joab and Abiathar, both of whom were once faithful to David. Adonijah prepared a coronation feast and invited his brothers and other royal officials.

7. David had taken an oath in the Lord's name, promising that Solomon would be king after him (1 Kings 1:30). God had favored Solomon already at his birth (2 Samuel 12:25) and had chosen him to build the temple (1 Chronicles 22:9–10), promising to establish David's throne through Solomon's line forever.

8. When Adonijah realized his cause was lost, he sought asylum by clinging to the "horns" of God's altar. (See study leaflet 8 for an explanation of this.) Solomon wisely showed self-restraint. He warned his brother and showed him compassion in much the same way David had treated his enemies.

Day 4 • 1 Kings 2:1–12

9. David's advice to Solomon: *Be strong. Show yourself a man. Pay attention to what God requires. Follow Him. Keep God's commands. Watch how you live. Walk faithfully before the Lord with all your heart and soul.* In all this, David urged Solomon to love God's Word and seek His will. Let volunteers comment on how these admonitions apply to them in specific instances.

10. **Challenge question.** When God forgives, He forgets. "For I will forgive their iniquity, and I will remember their sin no more" (Jeremiah 31:34b). Surely, David's redemption was complete. Because David was washed of his sin in the blood of the Savior who was to come, God could say of David that he did walk in God's ways and obey His commands, that he had lived with integrity and uprightness. This was God's evaluation of David's life.

11. (a) Encourage participants to share what they have written. If the group knows one another well, encourage them to tell what they will remember about one another. Talk about the spiritual legacy we leave with our children and other believers. (b) Let volunteers comment. Stress the power of the Holy Spirit to work sanctification in our lives.

Day 5 • 1 Kings 2:13–46

12. Adonijah may have fooled Bathsheba, but he could not fool Solomon, who saw through his ploy. Marriage to Abishag would greatly strengthen Adonijah's claim to the throne, because Abishag was considered part of David's harem. Solomon took drastic, but necessary, action in executing Adonijah. Adonijah had been given the chance to go home and live in peace. He refused. Solomon acted to put down further possible insurrection. He wisely chose not to murder Abiathar; instead, he deposed and banished him. By executing Joab, Solomon cleared his house of the guilt of the innocent blood Joab had shed throughout his life; Joab was guilty of more than one cold-blooded murder. Solomon's actions were justified and in keeping with his father's instructions. When Shimei refused to comply with Solomon's orders, he, too, lost his life. Solomon proved himself an able ruler who wisely dispensed both mercy and justice and knew when to use each. By acting as he did, he avoided having to devote time and attention to the kinds of insurgencies that plagued David's reign.

13. David (vv. 1–5; 14–16) made extensive preparations for the construction of the temple Solomon was

Small-Group Leaders Session 8   **Life of David**

to build. David (vv. 6–13) explained these preparations in great detail to Solomon and (v. 12) prayed for Solomon. David also (vv. 17–19) urged other leaders in the nation to respect and help Solomon. David could have done more to officially name Solomon as the nation's new king and to erase all doubt about Adonijah's fraudulent claim to power. But in other ways, David's plans seem quite extensive.

14. *For personal reflection. Sharing optional.* Let participants reflect and comment, if they wish. Answers will vary.

15. Take some time to share participants' responses. Use this question to look back at previous lessons and review the main points. You may want to pray together, thanking God for what you've learned.

David's Son, David's Lord

Selected Passages

Preparing for the Session

Central Focus

The promise of an eternal dynasty the Lord made to David is repeated time and again by Old Testament prophets and is ultimately fulfilled in Christ. Jesus Christ, David's Son yet David's Lord, will reign forever and ever. He provides a home for His people in His eternal kingdom, where we will no longer be disturbed or threatened.

Objectives

That participants, led by the Holy Spirit working through God's Word, will

1. understand that studying the life of David is not merely a historical or moral exercise, but essentially points us to Christ;

2. come to appreciate the numerous references to David made throughout Scripture; and

3. see themselves as beneficiaries of the Lord's promise to David.

For the Small-Group Leader

Small-Group Discussion Helps

Day 1 • 2 Samuel 7:4–16

1. (a) God called David from shepherding flocks of sheep to be shepherd over Israel. As a shepherd king, David would guard the peace and security of God's flock (v. 10), the people of Israel. (b) Solomon ruled Israel after David; he was David's "seed" or son (v. 12). Solomon (v. 13) built a "house" or temple for the Lord. God was Solomon's Father, despite Solomon's sins. God's mercy never left Solomon (v. 15), but He passed the kingdom of Israel (or part of it, Judah) on to Solomon's son Rehoboam to rule (v. 16). (c) Solomon could not rule David's kingdom forever (v. 13); no mortal human being could (see also v. 16). (d) Jesus was punished by human beings for our sins. Beaten and crucified, Jesus carried David's iniquity—as well as Solomon's and ours—the Son of David bore all human sin.

2. After condemning the under-shepherds, the false prophets and negligent priests of Israel in verses 1–10, Ezekiel goes on to prophesy about the Lord, the Good Shepherd who will search for His sheep, look after them, rescue them, gather the scattered, give them a home, provide for their needs, care for the injured and weak, and treat all of them justly.

3. (a) Ezekiel refers to great David's Greater Son, Jesus. This greater "David" is the Shepherd described in verses 11–16. Jesus Himself would tend His flock. (See number 2 above.) (b) In John 10, Jesus identifies Himself as this Good Shepherd, the one who lays down His own life for the sheep. (c) Into eternity, our Good Shepherd will guard His flock and provide the living water of eternal life for us. (d) Answers will vary.

Day 2 • 2 Samuel 7:4–16

4. In 2 Samuel 7:11b–13, God promised David He would build a house for David, a royal dynasty, that would last forever. In one sense, that dynasty began with David's son Solomon, who succeeded him; yet, in a deeper sense, God was promising to send Jesus to be His people's Shepherd, King, and Savior. Jesus would fulfill God's promises to David.

5. (a) The earthly kings who sat on the throne of David did not all prove loyal to the Lord. The kings of Judah would come under God's judgment for their lack of justice toward the oppressed, the fatherless, the widows, and the innocent; they would receive judgment for their idolatry and their selfish excesses. Their kingdom would therefore be toppled by the invading Babylonians, and the people would be taken into exile. (b) Nevertheless, God would keep His promise to David. God Himself would raise up a righteous Branch, a King who would "reign as king and deal wisely, and shall execute justice and righteousness in the land" (Jeremiah 23:5). His righteousness would be imputed to His subjects (Jeremiah 23:6).

6. (a) Jesus, David's descendant, came to earth to establish an eternal kingdom, not by military victories but by His own suffering and death so we could live

in righteousness with God forever. His incarnation and birth were the first steps in God's plan for "great David's greater Son." (b) Jesus wasn't the military conqueror the people had expected. His weakness, His "ordinariness" disappointed them. Then, too (John 7:14–24), many of them had hearts hardened by sin and self-righteousness. They did not *want* to obey God; this blinded them to Jesus' true identity and to the true righteousness He made available by God's grace (v. 17).

7. **Challenge question.** The Spirit of the Lord rested on both David (1 Samuel 16:13) and Jesus (Matthew 3:16). By God's grace, David wanted to do what pleased the Lord; but only Jesus obeyed God's will perfectly (John 8:29). David was known for his wisdom and compassion, for his power and might. Jesus also exercised wisdom in His teaching and in His responses to His opponents. Jesus demonstrated His power over nature, disease, and death; David had no such power.

8. Verses 6–10 remain to be fully realized. The peace these verses describe between human beings and the natural world will be fulfilled in the "new heaven and new earth" God has prepared for His children. War, hatred, pain, and injustice will disappear (v. 9). Believing Jews and Gentiles alike will experience His victory over sin and death as we rest forever in Him (v. 10).

9. (a) We belonged on the cross, not Jesus. We deserved punishment for our sins. He was sinless. Yet, He stood in our place; He was condemned and died the death that was ours. A great exchange, indeed! Surely, this is pure grace. (b) Encourage sharing. In response to God's grace, the Holy Spirit moves us to trust God; to love Him who first loved us; to worship, praise, and thank Him; to obey His Word; to serve God and others. Accept reasonable answers.

Day 3 • 2 Samuel 7:4–16

10. (a) God promised to maintain a loving, Father-son relationship with David and his descendants. In the Middle East, the relationship between a great king and the kings he had conquered was not only that of "lord" and "servant" but also of "father" and "son." See Psalm 2:7. (b) When Jesus was baptized, the heavenly Father announced to the world that Jesus was His Son, the Son who pleased Him fully.

11. (a) The people asked in Matthew 9:27 and 15:22 for physical healing. The Palm Sunday crowd cried, "Hosanna"—"Lord, save!" (b) **Challenge question.** Only the true "Son of David," the Messiah, could possibly do what was asked of Jesus. Some in Jesus' earthly time and place recognized Him for who He really was. Others, particularly the Palm Sunday worshipers, were looking for political deliverance. They abandoned Jesus when He disappointed them by allowing Himself to suffer and die. The prophets had made it clear the Messiah would come from David's line. This was well-known among the people of Israel. The "Son of David" was a popular Jewish title for the Messiah. Even among non-Jews, the title became well-known as news of Jesus' miracles spread far and wide. The Palm Sunday crowd and children in the temple called Jesus the "Son of David," indicating that they identified Him with the Messiah.

Day 4 • Various Passages

12. Luke makes it crystal clear that Jesus is the promised descendant of David, the Messiah. The angel states this at the annunciation (1:32–33). Zechariah sings of the Messiah in 1:69. He rejoices in the fulfillment of God's promise. The angels (2:11) announce the Savior's birth and connect it with the messianic promise to David. God wanted to make sure no honest doubts lingered in any inquirer's mind. Jesus was the Messiah God had sent.

13. **Challenge question.** Jesus' question pointed to the fact that the Messiah was more than a descendant of David. He was also David's *Lord*, just as Scripture had foretold. Unless Jesus' enemies were willing to admit that the Messiah was also the Son of God, they could not answer His question.

14. Encourage personal sharing. Stress that we are the beneficiaries of God's promise to David. This ancient promise, fulfilled when God sent His Son to be our Shepherd King, continues to bless all who believe Jesus is the Savior. We see clearly that God is faithful, reliable, true to His Word. We can put our trust in Him. God works through human life and history to accomplish *His* purposes. Nothing stands in His way. God works graciously and justly. He demonstrates His love for sinners. Jesus is our Shepherd King who guards and protects us here on earth and ushers us into the peace and safety of our heavenly home when life here is done.

Day 5 • Various Passages

15. (a) Peter makes the point that David was a prophet, inspired by the Holy Spirit when he wrote concerning Judas' betrayal and the need to replace him (Psalm

69:25; 109:8). (b) Peter points out that David prophesied about Christ's resurrection. Peter links "this Jesus, whom [they] crucified" (v. 36) with David's promised descendant (Psalm 16:8–11). (c) In his prayer, Peter acknowledges David's prophecy about the rebellion and opposition of faithless leaders against Jesus, the chosen Messiah (Psalm 2:1–2).

16. Paul identifies Jesus as the human descendant of David and, at the same time, the Son of God.

17. Paul quotes David in Psalm 32:1–2 to support his point that God justifies sinners by faith—crediting us with righteousness through faith in the Savior.

18. Jesus calls Himself the root and the descendant of David, and the bright morning star. Paul, in Romans 15:12, refers to Isaiah's prophecy (Isaiah 11:1, 10) about the root of Jesse. In the prophecy of Balaam (Numbers 24:17), the Messiah would arise as a star from Jacob to deliver Israel. Jesus was the Morning Star who completely fulfilled these prophecies, delivering His people from sin and death.

19. Allow participants to share what they have written. We may identify with David in some of the details of his earthly life. We, too, are chosen by God's grace and set purposefully on a path in this life. We, too, fall into sin and experience God's grace and mercy again and again. We, too, by the Spirit's power, learn to trust God's mercy. We love God, worship Him, and seek to serve Him. But more important, we identify with David because we are also his descendants. Jesus, David's descendant, has made us part of God's family. We share in the inheritance God promised David and delivered in His Son, Jesus Christ. By faith in Jesus, we enjoy everlasting life here in time and hereafter in the heavenly mansions, where we will live forever at peace in the family "home."

20. Invite participants to share their questions and insights. Close with a prayer of thanks for your growth together.